IMPLEMENTING
CRIMINAL JUSTICE POLICIES

Volume 26
SAGE RESEARCH PROGRESS SERIES IN CRIMINOLOGY

SAGE RESEARCH PROGRESS SERIES IN CRIMINOLOGY

Published in Cooperation with the American Society of Criminology
Series Editor: **MICHAEL R. GOTTFREDSON**, *State University of New York at Albany*
Founding Series Editor: **JAMES A. INCIARDI**, *University of Delaware*

SAGE RESEARCH PROGRESS SERIES IN CRIMINOLOGY
VOLUME 26

IMPLEMENTING CRIMINAL JUSTICE POLICIES

edited by MERRY MORASH

Published in cooperation with the
AMERICAN SOCIETY of CRIMINOLOGY

SAGE PUBLICATIONS
Beverly Hills / London / New Delhi

Copyright © 1982 by Sage Publications, Inc.

For information address:

SAGE Publications, Inc.
275 South Beverly Drive
Beverly Hills, California 90212

SAGE Publications India Pvt. Ltd.
C-236 Defence Colony
New Delhi 110 024, India

SAGE Publications Ltd
28 Banner Street
London EC1Y 8QE, England

Printed in the United States of America

Library of Congress Cataloging in Publication Data

Main entry under title:

Implementing criminal justice policies.

(Sage research progress series in criminology ;
v. 26)
    Includes bibliographies.
    Contents: Introduction / Merry Morash — The
Garnes Decree in reality : determining parole
eligibility for District of Columbia women /
Lucy Y. Steinitz — Implementing a national crime
control program / Joan Neff Gurney — [etc.]
    1. Criminal justice, Administration of — United
States — Addresses, essays, lectures. 2. Law
enforcement — United States — Addresses, essays,
lectures. I. Morash, Merry, 1946-   II. American
Society of Criminology. III. Series.
HV8141.I46   1982   364'973   82-10718
ISBN 0-8039-1884-4
ISBN 0-8039-1885-2 (pbk.)

FIRST PRINTING

CONTENTS

1

Merry Morash

Michigan State University

INTRODUCTION
Understanding Criminal Justice
Policy Implementation

The papers selected for this book exemplify a developing body of research on the often neglected process of implementing criminal justice policies. They describe research on law enforcement, court, and correctional policies that affect both the juvenile and adult systems. They identify several common implementation difficulties in the different criminal justice settings. Additionally, all of the chapters expose the dynamics through which national and state criminal justice policies are either translated into practice or subverted by various organizations, groups, or individuals. Thus, by identifying the salient influences on implementation in a large variety of criminal justice settings, they contribute to the development of theories to explain implementation outcome.

Theories to explain the causes of implementation success or failure are important for at least two practical reasons. First, if we know the common causes of implementation outcome, we can carry out feasibility studies to predict the likelihood that a particular policy will be implemented as desired (e.g., Bardach, 1977; Williams, 1976). Such a feasibility study may recommend crucial changes in the implementation plan to ensure the presence of factors related to successful implementation or to remove common barriers. When it is not possible to "stack the deck" in favor of implementation success, a feasibility study may recommend more viable alternative policies. The second practical use of knowledge of the causes of implementation outcome is as a guide in research to identify the existence of these causes during the initial stages of policy implementation. Thus type of research can alert policy implementors to potential barriers to implementation, and steps can be taken to overcome the barriers in time to realize the desired outcomes.

THE PREVALENCE OF IMPLEMENTATION FAILURE

Recent years have seen a tremendous investment of resources in the formulation and implementation of public policy in the criminal justice area. Legislative policy guided the "Great Society" programs of the 1960s, and many of these programs were intended to prevent and treat crime and delinquency. The "War on Crime" of the 1970s involved additional legislation to revamp the entire criminal justice system throughout the nation. The courts also have become more active in the development of judicial policy that impinges on criminal justice activities. For example, courts have attempted to protect criminal suspects' due process rights, and they have designed and supervised major institutional changes in order to improve prison conditions. Finally, in keeping with the political attention to social problems in general and to crime in particular, executive decisions frequently have reflected major criminal justice policies, as most recently evidenced by President Reagan's directive to reconsider the use of preventive detention for criminal suspects.

At the same time that national and state criminal justice policies have proliferated, there has been growing attention to failures in policy implementation. Policy implementation "encompasses those actions by public and private individuals (or groups) that affect the achievement of objectives set forth in prior policy decisions" (Van Horn and Van Meter, 1977: 103). Successful policy implementation does not require local organizations to duplicate completely the procedures and programs that are outlined in a policy. To the contrary, it may be necessary to adapt these procedures and programs to local conditions in order to achieve the intended outcome. However, the tendency toward using procedures and programs that actually make it impossible to achieve policy objectives suggests that such desirable adaptation of policy plans does not occur regularly.

There are numerous examples of failures in criminal justice policy implementation. Klein's (1979) review of an extensive collection of published and unpublished studies of the juvenile deinstitutionalization and diversion policies documented some of these failures: the use of inappropriate and unsystematic programs to achieve policy objectives; targeting of programs at inappropriate clients; too limited service variety and availability; and the location of programs in receptive environments rather than those most in need of change. In their case study of a plan to reorganize and professionalize the Dallas Police Department, Wycoff and Kelling (1978: 14) discussed an extreme type of implementation failure, projects that "simply never got off the ground." In another example, Feeley et al. (1977: 217) described different approaches to implementing the Safe Streets Act, which encouraged the development of state planning agencies (SPAs) to "plan for the rational development of a system of criminal justice." According to Feeley and his coauthors, the tendency of some SPAs to ignore the intent of the policy and take only the actions necessary to obtain federal funding has been a blatant example of implementation failure. A listing of such failures could continue indefinitely. When implementation failure occurs, we do not know if the policy itself could not bring about the desired social changes, or if the policy as incorrectly implemented accounted for the lack of desired changes. Thus, it is crucial to identify and explain failures not only to avoid them but to make some meaningful assessment of the worth of various policies.

RESEARCH ON IMPLEMENTATION

Several bodies of knowledge are pertinent to research on the causes of implementation failures. The political science literature is particularly helpful because it focuses on a broad range of influences for a wide variety of policies. The focus on a broad range of influences is consistent with the recognition that local community conditions, along with the local, state, and national interest groups and organizations, have important effects on criminal justice system operations (e.g., see Duffee, 1980). Moreover, the focus on different types of policies increases the chances that we can generalize the literature to our specific area of interest, criminal justice policy.

During the last decade, the political science literature on policy implementation has grown through two stages. In the first stage, a number of case studies were conducted to identify several important barriers to implementation. The case studies were of policies as diverse as New Town legislation to revitalize inner cities (Derthick, 1972), the Economic Development Administration's job program in Oakland, California (Pressman and Wildavsky, 1973), and Title V of the Elementary and Secondary Education Act (Murphy, 1973). In the second stage, there have been attempts at theory building, or modeling the implementation process, in order that common barriers to implementation can be revealed and studied with some consistency. The models do not focus on any particular type of policy, or on any particular setting. They integrate knowledge from several areas, most notably organization theory, research on the degree to which individuals impede organizational change, the literature on compliance with judicial orders and findings, and the literature on the diffusion, adoption, and application of both technology and program innovation.

Given the existence of several models of implementation, at this time it is appropriate to move to a third stage of research. At this third stage, studies can be conducted to test the strength of alternative models—or, more specifically, to identify the most common barriers to implementation.

There is very little research in this third stage that identifies the range and incidence of influences on criminal justice policy implementation and relates the identified influences back to general policy implementation models. As a notable exception, Wycoff and Kelling (1978) used a general model of implementation developed by Van Horn and Van Meter (1977) to explain the failure to implement major changes in the Dallas Police Department.[1] Additional studies are needed to demonstrate the utility of models of implementation when they are generalized to criminal justice settings. The remaining chapters of this book include such studies of the variables that the models identify as influences on implementation, as well as insightful examples and discussion of strategies for conducting the needed research.

A discussion of key political science and criminal justice literature serves as a good introduction to the chapters. This literature identifies a wide variety of possible effects on implementation and therefore is the backdrop against which we can see how these chapters fill gaps in research on the influences on criminal justice implementation. Political scientists' general models of implementation will be discussed first, followed by a review of literature on implementation of specific criminal justice policies.

GENERAL MODELS OF INFLUENCES ON IMPLEMENTATION

Although several political scientists have developed models to specify a range of influences on implementation, Van Horn and Van Meter's (1977) approach provides a particularly broad overview. The Van Horn-Van Meter model is based on their relatively recent compilation of organization theory literature. The model specifies eight general categories of variables, called "variable clusters," that can affect policy implementation. The first two clusters are (1) policy resources, most obviously money, and (2) standards for policy implementation. The standards are usually contained in legislation or in judicial or executive pronouncements, as well as in program regulations. Three additional variable clusters are (3) communication of the policy and standards, (4) methods used to enforce the standards, and (5) the disposition of people who work in the implementing agency to support the policy. The sixth variable cluster includes (6) characteristics of the implementing agency, such as staff competence and financial and political support. The seventh variable cluster includes (7) characteristics of the political environment, for example, public and elite opinion. The eighth variable cluster includes (8) economic and social conditions, such as the need for the program and for federal or state assistance.

There is considerable disagreement among political scientists about the relative influence of the different types of variables. Taking one position, Berman (1978: 77) found that factors within the organizations that were directly responsible for carrying out higher-level educational policies had the most influence on implementation outcome. These factors included "local organization's goals and agenda at the project's outset," the implementors' broad participation in planning, and "coalition building and bargaining for cementing bureaucratic commitments of managers." All of the variables identified by Berman fall into Van Horn and Van Meter's variable cluster, dispositions of people who work in the implementing agency to support the policy.

In contrast to Berman's strong emphasis on the local organization, or what is called the micro-level of implementation, Bardach (1977: 46) has stressed the macro-level by concluding that "implementation processes are driven at least as much if not more by the interorganizational transactions as by intraorganizational transactions." Bardach's own model of the forces affecting implementation focused on the interaction of such diverse groups and organizations as the "presumptive beneficiaries or clients," "private providers of goods and services," "regulatory agencies," and funding sources.

Not only is there disagreement about the relative influence of intraorganizational (micro-level) and interorganizational (macro-level) processes on implementation, but there is also disagreement about the relative influence of different kinds of variables at both levels. Sabatier and Mazmanian (1980) represent one position. Their model placed considerable emphasis on the legislative statute in which a policy is articulated. Concentrating on legislative regulatory policy, but not excluding other types, they hypothesized that a statute will be successfully implemented if, among other things, it incorporates a valid causal theory linking behavioral change to desired impacts and if implementation is assigned to agencies biased toward the statutory objective. In addition to such statutory character-istics, which fall into the Van Horn-Van Meter "standards for policy implementation" variable cluster, Sabatier and Mazmanian identified two other types of influence. The first of these is the nature of the problem to be solved by the policy. Policies will be easiest to implement if they address problems for which the solution is easily measured, that are solved by changing a limited variety of behavior to a limited extent, and that affect a small and easily identifiable target group. The second type of influence includes social, economic, and technological conditions; media attention; public support; and constituency group support. These overlap with the Van Horn-Van Meter political environment and economic and social condition variable clusters.

The Van Horn-Van Meter, Berman, and Sabatier-Mazmanian conceptual models of implementation are representative of several others (e.g., Naka-mura and Smallwood, 1980; Rein and Rabinowitz, 1978). Whereas the Van Horn-Van Meter model identified a broad range of general variable clusters, the others have included more specific variables and emphasized some of the clusters but not others.

Because the utility of the implementation models is to direct us to the empirical study of the effect of some of the many variables that might affect implementation, it is important to understand the variations between the different models. These emanate from several sources. First, the choice of predictive variables is due in part to the model originator's academic discipline. Organization theorists emphasize bureaucratic condi-tions; political scientists emphasize interest group pressures. Second, many of the models were developed inductively from case studies. Thus, the "relevant variables" are a function of the choice of case studies and the selective perceptions of those who carried out the studies. Third, the choice of variables is partly due to a focus on the macro-level (i.e., interorganizational/intergroup) of implementation as opposed to the micro-level (i.e., intraorganizational). As noted above, the two levels of implementation may differ in which variables have the major effect. Fourth, the choice of variables most certainly is influenced by the model builder's preferred theoretical framework. Describing different conceptual models resulting from various organization theories, Elmore (1978: 185-186) explains that the

> systems management model treats organizations as value-maximizing units and views implementation as an ordered, goal directed activity.

The bureaucratic process model emphasizes the roles of discretion and routine in organizational behavior and views implementation as a process of continually controlling discretion and changing routine. The organizational development model treats the needs of individuals for participation and commitment as paramount and views implementation as a process in which implementors shape policies and claim them as their own. The conflict and bargaining model treats organizations as arenas of conflict and views implementation as a bargaining process in which the participants converge on temporary solutions but no stable result is ever achieved.

For organization variables alone, each of these theoretical perspectives implies the importance of some but not other influences on implementation. Differing theories of individual and political behavior also suggest alternative sets of influential variables.

Given the assumption-laden and alternate models of policy implementation, it is reasonable to ask how such models can be of any use in understanding implementation in criminal justice settings. They are of use in alerting us to the need to test competing explanations of implementation outcome and to examine the theoretical assumptions implicit in any model. Additionally, the general models alert us to the range of possible influences on implementation and protect us from a myopic tendency to concentrate on a limited number of variables, which may or may not be the most important. In the next section, the Van Horn-Van Meter model will be used to discover those variables which are neglected and those which are emphasized in the research specific to criminal justice policy implementation.

INFLUENCES ON
CRIMINAL JUSTICE POLICY IMPLEMENTATION

Reports of empirical research and theoretical articles specific to criminal justice policy implementation are scattered throughout the political science, criminal justice, and occasionally the sociology publications. By comparing the wide range of influences on implementation identified by Van Horn and Van Meter with the influences considered by research focused on criminal justice policy, it was possible to identify emphases as well as gaps in the existing research.

The type of variable Van Horn and Van Meter identified and the one that has been most often emphasized in studies (Bardach, 1977; Moore, 1978; Lermack, 1977; Wice, 1974; Klein, 1979; Brintnall, 1979) of criminal justice policy implementation is the disposition of people who work in the implementing agency to support the policy. In one of the few conceptual discussions of the range of variables that affect criminal justice policy implementation, Musheno et al. (1976: 266) wrote:

> The extent to which public interest goals can be reached depends entirely on how well they serve the self-interests of those who are responsible for executing the policies in question.

Self-interests include desires to "win votes, expand power and authority, get more salary or higher budget, improve interpersonal relations" (Musheno et al., 1976: 267).[2]

Although it is questionable that the self-interests of implementors are always or exclusively the major influence on criminal justice policy implementation, there are circumstances when this conceptualization does seem accurate. Brintnall (1979) described such circumstances surrounding a federal policy to stimulate the prosecution of economic crimes by local prosecutors. The policy grew out of national pressure by elite, consumer-oriented interest groups. Local politics, however, had little influence on prosecutors' adoption of the policy, for several reasons. Economic crime was rarely a campaign issue; judges were not heavily involved in controlling economic crime; and the prosecutors obtained funds that were not controlled by any local group. The form of each prosecutor's economic crime unit, as a result, depended almost entirely on his or her personal disposition. Even though this extreme insulation of immediate policy implementors is not consistently found throughout the criminal justice system, a rather high degree of discretion and insulation does characterize the system. The prevalence of discretionary decision making probably does make the disposition of agency personnel to implement policy particularly important in criminal justice settings, as opposed to settings where behavior is more easily observed and restricted.

Unclear, diffuse, or contradictory standards, which is another of the variable types identified by Van Horn and Van Meter, also has been emphasized in the criminal justice policy literature (e.g., Feeley et al., 1977; Klein, 1979; Attewell and Gerstein, 1979; Dunbar, 1976; Wycoff and Kelling, 1978). Interviews by Feeley and his coauthors, for example, illustrated that "ambiguity, uncertainty, and frustration are characteristic of the way in which SPA (State Planning Agency) officials think about the mandates and intentions of the Safe Streets Act." In their case study of methadone maintenance programs, Attewell and Gerstein (1979) similarly demonstrated that standards prohibiting services to young heroin users who had not previously attended drug rehabilitation programs directly conflicted with the policy intent of controlling the spread of heroin use. The young and relatively inexperienced users who were barred from services were the most likely to introduce friends to the drug. Klein (1979), in another example of problems stemming from policy standards, found that the failure of the juvenile deinstitutionalization legislation to define the term "status offender" made policy implementation unlikely.

Since there is no empirical evidence of the frequency of unclear or contradictory criminal justice policy standards, or the strength of their relationship to implementation failure, we do not know that the emphasis on standards is justified. However, given the nature of criminal justice policymaking, standards probably are an important causal factor. Frequently, the national and state legislative policies that seek to influence criminal justice practices are the result of heated moral debate over the handling of offenders or justice to victims. Policy statements, therefore, are often compromises or modifications of proposed legislation. The details of standards may be omitted or left ambiguous or even contradictory to the policy intent in order to avoid inflaming disagreements.

The variables in the Van Horn-Van Meter category, characteristics of the implementing agency, have been considered in some criminal justice policy implementation literature, although not to the extent of the variables related to implementors' dispositions and policy standards. Lewis and Greene's (1978) general model of policy implementation is relevant to understanding the influence of the characteristics of the implementing agency. They identified two agency characteristics that affect implementation success: clarity regarding goals and functions and consensus concerning the intent of the policy. Moore's (1978) description of the international drug supply reduction policy before the establishment of the Drug Enforcement Administration exemplifies the effects of clarity regarding goals and functions and consensus regarding policy intent. The State Department was expected to pressure foreign governments to curtail drug supplies, and the Bureau of Narcotics and Dangerous Drugs (BNDD) staff were to serve as law enforcement advisors to the foreign countries. These activities were not consistent with the goals and functions of either agency. The State Department's primary goal was to maintain working relationships with foreign governments, which was at odds with pressuring foreign governments. BNDD was a law enforcement agency with the goal of prosecuting criminal cases; the law enforcement advisor role was inconsistent with solving crimes and making arrests. Because law enforcement, the courts, and correctional organizations ultimately facilitate or block policy, they deserve consistent attention in the criminal justice policy literature. The Lewis and Greene (1978) model and Moore's (1978) research illustrate the need to focus implementation research on characteristics of the implementing agency.

Like agency characteristics, communication failures have received some but not extensive emphasis as potential blocks to criminal justice policy implementation (e.g., Wycoff and Kelling, 1978: 62). Research has documented that judicial policies are particularly subject to communication impediments, since courts do not have a routine way to inform institutions or lower courts, besides those directly involved in a case, of their findings. Wasby's (1970) seminal discussion of the Miranda ruling to protect the due process rights of criminal suspects illustrated the problem. The complicated rationale behind the ruling was usually overlooked in the media, and Miranda was presented not as a necessary protection against police abuse but as a major restraint on law enforcement activities. Police who had learned of the Miranda ruling primarily from the media tended to disapprove of it, most likely as a result of this communication distortion. It is unlikely that these disapproving police would act to implement the ruling fully.

The first of the influences identified by Van Horn and Van Meter, limited policy resources, is rarely mentioned in the literature on criminal justice policy implementation. An exception is found in Feeley et al. (Feeley et al., 1977: 216), who pointed out that criminal justice State Planning Agencies controlled only two or three percent of each state's criminal justice expenditure. As a result, it was difficult for them to carry out the extensive revamping of legal institutions as was mandated by the Safe Streets Act. The relative de-emphasis on resources is questionable, for the situation of limited funds and a mandate for comprehensive reform, which is described by Feeley et al., is common in the criminal justice system.

With the possible exception of research using a compliance or cost-benefit approach (e.g., Nagel and Neef, 1979), very little attention is paid to the Van Horn-Van Meter cluster of variables representing methods used to enforce policy standards. These methods can include monitoring, monetary and other incentives, sanctions, and education. Because Wycoff and Kelling (1978) systematically located examples of the Van Horn-Van Meter categories of influences on implementation, they provided one of the few examples of this problem. They noted that within the Dallas Police Department the subsection charged with implementing the reorgani-

zation plan had no way to provide sanctions or incentives to line supervisors. Thus enforcement was not possible. The spotty attention to
methods to enforce standards in criminal justice settings is unfortunate,
for enforcement is one of the few variables that can be manipulated to
maximize the chances that a policy will be implemented.

Probably the most consistently neglected influences on criminal justice
policy implementation are the last two of the Van Horn-Van Meter
variable clusters, the political environment and economic and social conditions. Although there are exceptions to the neglect (e.g., Grau, 1981;
Lewis and Greene, 1978; Wycoff and Kelling, 1978), there is a tendency to
focus on the micro-level of implementation and in so doing direct attention to the implementing agency and its staff rather than to the larger
environment. Even when macro-level implementation is considered, the
focus usually has been on relations with the federal agencies rather than
other groups that are in the environment of local implementors. Given the
fragmentation and interdependence of law enforcement, the courts, and
correctional agencies, it is essential to consider the larger environment.
Grau (1981) underscored this point in a case study of an attempted
sentencing reform, the use of community restitution in Austin. He found
the following:

> At the systemic level, the planned sentencing reform in Austin
> threatened prosecutorial hegemony over sentencing, which was rein-
> forced by the interests of the court in maintaining fine revenue, of
> the judges in promoting career advancement, of the bar in protecting
> the sentence and plea negotiation process and minimizing clients'
> sentences, and of the probation department in maintaining the flow
> of revenue from its caseloads [Grau, 1981: 96].

In Austin, the political stance of a variety of groups outside of the
implementing agency mitigated against the use of community restitution
dispositions.

Just as Grau brought attention to the often ignored political environment, Wycoff and Kelling (1978) brought it to social and environmental
variables. In the Dallas Police Department reorganization they described,
the social conditions impinging on implementation were citywide disagreement about the need for Dallas to plan for change versus a need to rectify
a city image damaged by the Kennedy assassination; a suspicion of outside
influences in the Texas city; and racial tensions that drew resources and
energy away from the implementation of the plan.

To summarize the discussion provided above, there is ample evidence that a tremendous range of variables, generally represented by the Van Horn-Van Meter categories, are relevant to criminal justice implementation. Although some of these variables are presented as more important than others in the literature, there is reason to question the emphasis. Several studies have demonstrated that the most neglected variables seem to be quite important in some settings.

A study by Downs and Rocke (1979) stands out because it directly addressed the issue of which variables are most important. They examined the effects of a large number of both organizational variables and selected social environment and political conditions on the degree of implementation of the juvenile justice deinstitutionalization policy in 50 states. They found that socioeconomic conditions in the state were less related to degree of implementation than either agency director's ideology or agency autonomy (1979: 725). Agency director's ideology and autonomy were the most predictive of the organizational variables affecting implementation. The effect of the director's ideology was much stronger when agency autonomy was high than when it was low. Their finding provides strong support for the emphasis in the literature on the effect of self-interest on implementation. However, it should be noted that this variable was most predictive in combination with an aspect of the political environment, specifically agency autonomy.

IMPLICATIONS FOR RESEARCH

The above review of selected criminal justice policy implementation studies has three clear implications for needed research, and thus for the contribution of the articles in this book. First, since we have been able to illustrate the operation of all of a wide range of variables identified in general models of implementation, we are certainly not in a position to rule out some types in future studies. Thus, additional case studies can be instructive. Case studies can continue the identification of the range of specific variables that affect policy implementation in a variety of criminal justice settings. This process provides empirical support for the importance of the variables which the models identify.

The second implication of the review pertains to the relative salience of different variables as influences on implementation. Here the information is sparse. At best we can infer that one variable is more salient than another from our general knowledge of the criminal justice system. Ambiguous standards and standards that are inconsistent with the intent of a policy are likely to result from the heated moral debate surrounding criminal justice policy formulation. Thus, ambiguous and inconsistent standards are likely to be important influences on criminal justice policy implementation. Self-interest of implementors also is likely to be important in criminal justice settings, given the decentralization and discretionary nature of the criminal justice agencies. The interdependence among criminal justice agencies is a reason to expect interorganizational politics to be particularly important, too. Although other, frequently unstudied variables cannot be ruled out as probable hindrances to criminal justice policy implementation, variables related to standards, individuals' disposition, and interorganizational politics can certainly be "ruled in."

OVERVIEW OF THE VOLUME

The chapters in this book go beyond and reinforce existing research on criminal justice police implementation in several ways. The first six articles are case studies of implementation in diverse criminal justice settings and at both the micro- and macro-levels.

In the first case study, Steinitz examines implementation of the Garnes decree. This decree was intended to allow District of Columbia female prisoners to serve part of their sentences in the District of Columbia rather than in distant federal prisons. In direct contradiction to the intent of the decree, the implementing agencies, the U.S. Parole Commission and the District of Columbia Department of Corrections instituted procedures that resulted in more lengthy sentences for the women and more time served outside the District. Steinitz attributes the implementation failure to a variable that is sometimes neglected in criminal justice research: the lack of communication between agencies. Consistent with previous research, a lack of specificity in the decree standards further contributed to implementation failure.

Also focusing on the transfer of a policy from a national to a local level, Gurney shows that the goals of the policy to prosecute economic crimes affecting disadvantaged groups are subverted by local prosecutors' immediate goals of obtaining lengthy records of convictions. Ironically, the original policy intent of helping disadvantaged groups was inverted by procedures leading to increased criminal prosecution of members of disadvantaged groups. The effect of the important variables, characteristics of the implementing agency, and related self-interest of the implementors (prosecutors) is well illustrated.

In his study of a state policy for mandatory sentencing of criminals who use guns, Bynum similarly demonstrates the local subversion of policy goals. He shows that despite clear policy directives and an apparent commitment of key individuals, environmental pressures and constraints influenced prosecutors to apply the mandatory sentencing policy selectively and in some cases to apply it selectively to minority offenders. In the prosecutors' offices he studied, local political conditions were more salient influences on the implementation than were original policy standards or state-level support. The frequent neglect of such local environmental factors in research is rectified in Bynum's study.

Zalman's thought-provoking work provides additional interpretation of Bynum's findings regarding the Michigan gun control legislation. Zalman insists that the discretionary and incomplete application of the legislation results from an intended ambiguity in the standard and from legislators' political interests. By extending the case study of the Michigan gun control legislation into the past, Zalman also extends our understanding of the source of implementation failure.

Consistent with his implementation model (Lewis and Greene, 1978), described earlier, Greene reveals that the successful use of special police units depends on both characteristics of the police agency (e.g., goal consensus) and the unit's relations with external organizations. Furthermore, the most effective method for enforcing successful implementation depends on the structure of relations between the special police unit and those agencies that use the unit's services. Greene's study is unique in its consideration of the interaction between methods for enforcement and organizational structure, as well as in its consideration of these often overlooked variables at all.

Blakely and Davidson report their finding that the failure to implement a diversion program resulted from staff dispositions toward legalistic interactions with youths rather than the intended delivery of advocacy and recreational services. When all other variables were controlled through an experimental design, staff disposition proved influential. This finding is highly consistent with prior research to show the critical nature of the staff disposition variable.

The final two chapters in this volume are not case studies, but instead consider the utility of research on criminal justice policy implementation. Decker's contribution demonstrates the use of process evaluation results as feedback to implementing agencies. In his example, the evaluation results show that social service and police staff involved in a juvenile diversion policy have the goal consensus required for successful implementation.

Huff and Alpert explore the role of evaluation research in assessing and obtaining compliance with judicial decrees aimed at correctional institutions.

Together, the chapters in this book document important influences on implementation that have been relatively ignored in prior criminal justice research, though they were identified in general models. These previously neglected influences include communication among agencies, local environmental pressures and constraints on the implementing agency, local agency characteristics such as goal consensus, and methods of enforcing policies. Our knowledge of the criminal justice system suggested that they would be important influences on implementation, and the case studies confirm their importance.

The chapters also reinforce prior findings that both the quality of policy standards and the disposition of implementing agency staff to support the policy are influential factors. Along with prior research, these studies identify a number of variables that should be considered in feasibility studies of implementation, in process evaluations of the implementation process, and in future tests of theoretical models of the causes of criminal justice policy implementation outcome.

NOTES

1. The Dallas Police Department plan was a department policy linked through Law Enforcement Assistance Administration funding to national policies to professionalize the police, and also influenced by the Police Foundation, which provided a private source of funding.

2. It should be noted that in a more recent publication (Levine et al., 1980: 481-482) Musheno, Palumbo, and Levine identify other influences on implementation, such as adequacy of information, resources, and communication. They do, however, continue to stress the overriding effect of self-interest and, in some cases, group interest.

REFERENCES

ATTEWELL, P. and D. R. GERSTEIN (1979) "Government policy and local practice." Amer. Soc. Rev. 44 (April): 311-327.

BARDACH, E. (1977) The Implementation Game. Cambridge: MIT Press.

BERMAN, P. (1978) "The study of macro- and micro-implementation." Public Policy 26 (Spring): 157-184.

BRINTNALL, M. A. (1979) "Federal influence and urban policy entrepreneurship in the local prosecution of economic crime." Policy Studies J. 7 (Spring): 577-592.

DERTHICK, M. (1972) New Towns In-Town: Why a Federal Program Failed. Washington, DC: Urban Institute.

DOWNS, G. and D. ROCKE (1979) "Bureaucracy and juvenile corrections in the states." Policy Studies J. 7 (Summer): 721-728.

DUFFEE, D. E. (1980) Explaining Criminal Justice. Cambridge, MA: Oelgeschlager, Gunn and Hain.

DUNBAR, E. R. (1976) Organizational Change and the Politics of Bureaucracy: Illustrations from the Initiation of Mutual Agreement Programming in Three State Correctional Agencies. College Park, MD: American Correctional Association.

ELMORE, R. F. (1978) "Organizational models of social program implementation." Public Policy 26 (Spring): 185-228.

FEELEY, M. M., A. SARAT, and S. O. WHITE (1977) "The role of state planning in the development of criminal-justice federalism," pp. 204-224 in J. A. Gardiner (ed.) Public Law and Public Policy. New York: Praeger.

GRAU, C. W. (1981) "The limits of planned change in courts." Justice System J. 6 (Spring): 84-99.

KLEIN, M. W. (1979) "Deinstitutionalization and diversion of juvenile offenders: a litany of impediments," pp. 145-202 in N. Morris and M. Tonry (eds.) Crime and Justice: An Annual Review of Research. Chicago: Univ. of Chicago Press.

LERMACK, P. (1977) "Hookers, judges, and bail forfeiters: the importance of internally generated demands on policy-implementing institutions." Admin. and Society 8 (February): 459-468.

LEVINE, J. P., M. C. MUSHENO, and D. J. PALUMBO (1980) Criminal Justice: A Public Policy Approach. New York: Harcourt Brace Jovanovich.

LEWIS, R. G. and J. P. GREENE (1978) "Implementation evaluation: a future direction in project evaluation." J. of Criminal Justice 6 (Summer): 167-176.

MOORE, M. H. (1978) "Reorganization plan # 2 reviewed: problems in implementing a strategy to reduce the supply of drugs to illicit markets in the United States." Public Policy 26 (Spring): 229-262.

MURPHY, J. T. (1973) "The education bureaucracies implement novel policy: the politics of Title 1 of ESEA, 1967-72," pp. 160-198 in A. P. Sindler (ed.) Policy and Politics in America. Boston: Little, Brown.

MUSHENO, M., D. PALUMBO, and J. LEVINE (1976) "Evaluating alternatives in criminal justice: a policy-impact model." Crime and Delinquency 22 (July): 265-283.

NAGEL, S. S. and M. G. NEEF (1979) Decision Theory and the Legal Process. Lexington, MA: D. C. Heath.

NAKAMURA, R. T. and F. SMALLWOOD (1980) The Politics of Policy Implementation. New York: St. Martin's.

PRESSMAN, J. L. and A. WILDAVSKY (1973) Implementation. Berkeley: Univ. of California Press.

REIN, M. and F. F. RABINOVITZ (1978) "Implementation: a theoretical perspective," pp. 307-335 in W. D. Burnham and M. W. Weinberg (eds.) American Politics and Public Policy. Cambridge: MIT Press.

SABATIER, P. and D. MAZMANIAN (1980) "The implementation of public policy: a framework of analysis." Policy Studies J. 8 (Special Issue 2): 538-560.

VAN HORN, C. E. and D. S. VAN METER (1977) "The implementation of intergovernmental policy," pp. 97-120 in S. S. Nagel (ed.) Policy Studies Review Annual, Vol. I. Beverly Hills, CA: Sage.

WASBY, S. L. (1970) The Impact of the United States Supreme Court: Some Perspectives. Homewood, IL: Dorsey Press.

WICE, P. B. (1974) Freedom for Sale: A National Study of Pretrial Release. Lexington, MA: D. C. Heath.

WILLIAMS, W. (1976) "Implementation analysis and assessment," pp. 267-292 in W. Williams and R. F. Elmore (eds.) Social Program Implementation. Beverly Hills, CA: Sage.

WYCOFF, M. A. and G. L. KELLING (1978) The Dallas Experience: Organizational Reform. Washington, DC: Police Foundation.

2

Lucy Y. Steinitz

Jewish Family and Children's Service,
Baltimore, Maryland

THE GARNES DECREE IN REALITY
Determining Parole Eligibility
for District of Columbia Women

In the District of Columbia, both District of Columbia (D.C.) and United States (U.S.) code violators are committed to the custody of the Attorney General of the United States. The District of Columbia has no facilities for holding long-term female offenders, although it does for long-term male offenders. Thus, the Federal Bureau of Prisons confines women serving terms in excess of one year in one of four federal correctional facilities: Alderson, West Virginia; Lexington, Kentucky; Fort Worth, Texas; or Pleasanton, California. The closest of these facilities to the District of Columbia is Alderson (300 miles away). In September 1980, this facility held 98 D.C. code violators (out of 122 total) and 24 U.S. code violators (out of 34) from the District of Columbia.

Women serving less than one year usually remain in the D.C. jail and are under the jurisdiction of the District of Columbia Department of Corrections (DCDC). The D.C. Board of Parole automatically handles all aspects of their parole release and supervision. Since D.C. women serving more than one year are on federal property (and therefore under federal jurisdiction), their parole situation is both unusual and complicated.

AUTHOR'S NOTE: The investigative research on which this chapter is based was conducted while I was a Research Fellow at the University of Chicago's Center for the Study of Welfare Policy in Washington, D.C., 1980-1981.

THE GARNES DECREE

In 1972, a civil action suit was brought by Lana Phoebe Garnes, an Alderson inmate, against Patricia Taylor, the District of Columbia's Department of Corrections Assistant Director for Women's Programs. Originally the suit sought to have the court declare unconstitutional the transfer of D.C. female offenders to federal prisons which are located hundreds of miles from their homes. The plaintiff dismissed the action in 1976, however, when both parties agreed on a joint stipulation for the improved designation referral and transfer of D.C. women offenders to and from Federal Bureau of Prisons facilities. This stipulation, which is known as the Garnes Decree, established a nine-month parole eligibility cut-off for determining federal versus District of Columbia jurisdiction. Specifically, the decree required the following of the Federal Bureau of Prisons:

(1) Refer to DCDC for transfer any D.C. woman in its custody who makes a voluntary request and is within nine months of her parole eligibility, expiration, or mandatory release date.[1]

(2) Designate to federal institutions most female D.C. code violators with sentences of more than one year who are not within nine months of a parole eligibility, expiration, or mandatory release date.

WHAT THESE PROCEDURES MEAN

Under District of Columbia law, the D.C. Board of Parole has jurisdiction over prisoners confined in penal institutions located in the District of Columbia, including both D.C. code violators and U.S. code violators. In federal correctional institutions, jurisdiction over D.C. and U.S. code violators is held by the U.S. Parole Commission. Thus, transfer under the Garnes Decree from a federal prison to a D.C. facility (e.g., halfway house or jail) means that the offender is heard by the D.C. Board of Parole, rather than by the U.S. Parole Commission. However, in order to ensure that an offender's transfer to the District of Columbia occurs only when her imminent release and supervision are assured, the Garnes Decree determined that for each D.C. offender who requests a transfer, DCDC must review a referral packet nine months piror to her parole eligibility, expiration, or mandatory release date. This packet, which is sent from the Bureau of Prisons to DCDC, must contain the following information and materials about the inmate:

(1) sentence data;

(2) presentence report when available;

(3) a progress report completed less than 90 days prior to the referral. (In addition to information concerning the offender's institutional adjustment and progress, the report should contain current information on outstanding detainers,[2] parole and prerelease eligibility status, and the offender's medical condition and psychological condition, if known); and

(4) for any D.C. woman committed for a violent offense or who has a prior record which includes a violent offense, a psychiatric or psychological report completed not more than 90 days prior to the referral.

In those cases where DCDC decides that it would either parole or supervise the mandatory release of the offender, the woman is subsequently transferred to Washington, D.C. and either paroled directly or placed in a work-release program (i.e., halfway house). The Garnes Decree requires that DCDC advise the Bureau of Prisons of its decision on each transfer request within 30 days of its receipt.

WHAT ACTUALLY OCCURS?

Information on how the Garnes Decree is actually implemented was derived from repeated cycles of in-depth telephone and personal interviews with 23 key administrators over a six-month period, January-June, 1981. Although no aggregate statistics are compiled by DCDC or the prisons, it was clear from these interviews that most long-term D.C. women prisoners seek a transfer to a D.C. facility under the provisions of the Garnes Decree for three major reasons. First, the D.C. Board of Parole is more likely than the U.S. Parole Commission to grant parole after the completion of a minimum sentence (i.e., at the parole eligibility date set at sentencing). By contrast, the U.S. Parole Commission usually extends the minimum sentence by several months or years, based on a system of salient factors used to determine parole eligibility. This system considers the prisoner's prior record, type of offense, and offender characteristics but does not include an assessment of either the prisoner's institutional behavior or her original parole eligibility date set at sentencing. Second, inmates learn that the D.C. Board of Parole tends to provide less supervision and a greater flexibility than the U.S. Parole Commission in the enforcement of parole requirements. While there are more regulations under the D.C. system, the large caseloads (approximately 80 to 85 per parole officer) render close supervision very difficult. In comparison, the U.S. Parole Commission averages 45 cases per officer and generally demands far more from each offender (e.g., urine samples, home visits, counseling sessions, training, and employment). Finally, transfer to a D.C. facility would bring these women, most of whom have young children, closer to their homes and families.

Problems in the transfer process began emerging four years ago when the U.S. Parole Commission started holding preliminary hearings at each federal facility, soon after each inmate arrived. According to Alderson's Executive Assistant to the Warden, the purpose was to inform all inmates immediately of their standing in relation to parole eligibility and release. For female offenders from the District of Columbia, however, this new procedure produces a negative impact. It means that D.C. women are heard by the U.S. Parole Commission within their first few weeks at the federal prison, *long before* the date when their referral packets are supposed to be sent to DCDC for consideration of a transfer. Thus, these offenders face the probability that the U.S. Parole Commission will grant them a *new date* (called the "presumptive parole date") that is *considerably later* than the original parole eligibility date set at sentencing. DCDC tends to rely on this new date—rather than on the original parole eligibility date—when considering an inmate's request for transfer to a District of Columbia facility. Thus, under these new circumstances, the earliest date at which D.C. women could expect to have their transfer requests approved would be postponed by the length of time their sentences are extended.

For example, take the hypothetical case of a woman at a federal prison whose parole eligibility has been set by a District of Columbia judge at two years. According to the Garnes Decree, she should be able to request a transfer to a D.C. facility nine months prior to her parole eligibility date (i.e., 15 months after she was sentenced). However, at the federal prison she is heard by the U.S. Parole Commission and receives a presumptive parole date of two years and ten months. As a result, the earliest date that DCDC would accept her request for transfer is also delayed by ten months (i.e., to 25 months after she was sentenced).

Persons disagreeing with this analysis argue that D.C. women have the option of not appearing before the U.S. Parole Commission prior to their referral to DCDC and the D.C. Board of Parole. Technically, this is true. However, as Alderson's Executive Assistant to the Warden pointed out, "That is very difficult for a woman to do when all her friends (i.e., fellow prisoners) are going before the Commission and getting some definite answers about where they stand." In addition, DCDC almost always refuses to grant a woman's transfer request unless she has first been heard by the U.S. Parole Commission. When asked to discuss the influence of the U.S. Parole Commission hearings on DCDC's transfer determination,

DCDC's Assistant Director for Women's Programs and Community Services explained that when a woman chooses not to appear before the U.S. Parole Commission, DCDC becomes suspicious that "she had something to hide." Transfer requests that come to DCDC without a U.S. Parole Commission decision are usually turned down with explanations such as "poor prison adjustment" or "needs more observation." In most cases the offender may resubmit her request to transfer nine months prior to the presumptive parole date which she receives at a U.S. Parole Commission hearing.

Of particular importance to understanding the reason for failure in the Garnes Decree implementation, the interviews revealed that the DCDC and the Alderson staff differ radically in terminology, standards, and procedures. Employees in the two departments know little or nothing about how the other system works. In preparing this report, this became evident in two ways. First, language varied so widely that terms used by some respondents (such as "D.C. statutory parole date" or "parole file") were completely unknown to others. To obtain clarity, respondents were asked to define the terms they used, with the result that even the same terms held different meanings. Still other terms had unique definitions. Although, for example, DCDC relies heavily on what they call the "presumptive parole eligibility date" in their decision making (termed "presumptive parole date" in this report, as used by the U.S. Parole Commission), the DCDC term appears neither in the Garnes Decree, nor in the Uniform Parole Reports of the National Council on Crime and Delinquency, nor at the National Criminal Justice Reference Service of the National Institute on Justice.

As a second indicator of the lack of interorganizational communication, none of the study respondents had a complete picture of what happens to the D.C. women from the time they receive their sentences through their parole. Essentially, staff at Alderson do not understand the procedures used by DCDC, and staff in the District have only a vague knowledge of what the women face at Alderson (and, to a lesser extent, in other federal facilities). The study respondents provided anecdotes of cases that got lost or were delayed due to some minor technicality or else were shuttled back and forth several times between the federal facility and DCDC before any transfer decision was made.

CONCLUSIONS

Nowhere in the Garnes Decree is any mention made of the U.S. Parole Commission's influence on DCDC's consideration of transfer of parole.

Yet, DCDC's reliance on the U.S. Parole Commission hearings has essentially rendered the Garnes Decree meaningless. This reliance denies equity for D.C. women offenders, as most D.C. male offenders do not undergo U.S. Parole Commission hearings (i.e., the District of Columbia has its own long-term correctional facility for men which is not under federal jurisdiction). It also places female D.C. code violators in the position of having to satisfy two distinct sets of standards. D.C. women must meet the standards of both the U.S. Parole Commission and the D.C. Board of Parole, while women prisoners in the 50 states have only their local state, county, or city parole boards with which to contend. Reliance by DCDC on U.S. Parole Commission hearings tends to lengthen the period of incarceration for D.C. women, which adds to the total cost of incarceration paid by the District of Columbia. Most important, the offenders' families and young children may experience irreparable harm from the prolonged separation, as has been shown in several studies on children of incarcerated mothers (Baunach, 1979; Gressani, 1976; McGowan and Blumenthal, 1978; Sametz, 1980).

The failure to implement the Garnes Decree is due partly to the nature of the relationship between the Federal Bureau of Prisons, of which Alderson is a part, and the District of Columbia Department of Corrections. The failure also results from a lack of specificity in the Garnes Decree regarding the process to be used in reaching decisions once the decree is in effect.

UPDATE AND RECOMMENDATIONS

The findings described here were first made public in a 1981 report by the University of Chicago's Center for the Study of Welfare Policy (Steinitz, n.d.). In response to that report, inquiries and follow-up were conducted through the Female Offender Network[3] and two interagency meetings[4] involving both the District of Columbia Department of Corrections and the Federal Bureau of Prisons. As a result, the Federal Bureau of Prisons agreed to draft a memorandum of understanding to be signed by the District of Columbia Department of Corrections and themselves. Three major recommendations were incorporated from the original report into this memorandum, which was mailed to DCDC on September 30, 1981 for further comment.

The first and central recommendation contained in the memorandum was that hearings by the U.S. Parole Commission should be entirely voluntary for D.C. women offenders in federal prisons. Second, the memorandum stated that the absence of a U.S. Parole Commission decision would not be considered a basis for denying a D.C. woman's request for transfer to the District of Columbia Department of Corrections. The third recommendation was that the Federal Bureau of Prisons and the District of Columbia Department of Corrections work together to develop clearly and concisely written procedures for implementing and monitoring the Games Decree. These recommendations and the interaction leading to their development could provide for fuller implementation of the Games Decree. However, it remains to be seen whether these steps alone can overcome obstacles to implementation.

NOTES

1. *Parole eligibility date:* the earliest date a person can be released to community supervision, as determined by statute or the sentencing judge. (In the District of Columbia, the parole eligibility date is usually set at one-third of the sentence. See Title 24, Section 204 of the D.C. Code.)

Expiration date: the final, last date of the maximum sentence, with no days off for "good time" (days off the maximum that a prisoner earns for satisfactory behavior).

Mandatory release date: the date the prisoner is released to community supervision as a result of good time or other statutory sentence reduction measures.

2. A "detainer" is a request lodged by another jurisdiction to put a hold on that person if he or she has pending charges in another jurisdiction.

3. The Female Offender Network, founded in 1979, holds quarterly forums and disseminates information to professionals and laypersons in the Washington, D.C. area who are interested in issues affecting female offenders.

4. June 24, 1981 and August 4, 1981.

REFERENCES

BAUNACH, P. J. (1979) The Separation of Inmate Mothers From Their Children. Final Report. Washington, DC: Law Enforcement Assistance Administration.
GRESSANI, A. (1976) "Mothers inside; children outside: a look at the relationship of incarcerated women offenders and their children." (mimeo)
McGOWAN, B. G. and K. BLUMENTHAL (1978) Why Punish the Children? A Study of Women Prisoners. Hackensack, NJ: National Council on Crime and Delinquency.
SAMETZ, L. (1980) "Children of incarcerated women." Social Work 25 (July): 298-302.

STEINITZ, L. Y. (n.d.) The Garnes Decree in Reality: Parole Eligibility and Determination for D.C. Women in Federal Correctional Institutions. Washington, DC: Center for the Study of Welfare Policy. (mimeo)

3

Joan Neff Gurney

University of Richmond

IMPLEMENTING A NATIONAL
CRIME CONTROL PROGRAM
The Case of an Economic
Crime Unit

This chapter examines the manner in which a local law enforcement agency implemented a national crime control program. The major thesis is that the goals of a national project can easily become subordinated to the more immediate concerns of the local agency charged with carrying them out. This theme is developed from findings of a study conducted on a local economic crime unit (ECU). The ECU was part of a nationwide project for which the goal was to increase the effectiveness of economic crime prosecution at the local level. The chapter documents that the aims of the national project were translated into goals more closely allied with the purposes of the local sponsoring agency, a county prosecutor's office.

BACKGROUND OF THE ECONOMIC CRIME PROJECT

The Economic Crime Project (ECP) was established in 1973 by the National District Attorneys Association in cooperation with the Batelle Human Affairs Research Center. An initial LEAA grant of $532,175 was used to set up an ECP coordinating office, first located in Washington, D.C. and later moved to Chicago. Fifteen prosecutors' offices were selected initially as pilot projects.[1]

Since its inception the project has expanded to include over 70 participating offices throughout the country. To date, over $5 million in LEAA

33

funds has been spent, with most used to staff and maintain the national coordinating headquarters. The headquarters staff provide information and assistance to local units, coordinate regional and national meetings among unit chiefs, and maintain liaisons with federal agencies directly or indirectly concerned with various forms of economic crime.[2] However, the local ECUs operate autonomously, for the most part, without close supervision from the national headquarters. They are located within and operate as part of county prosecutors' offices or metropolitan district attorneys' offices.

The general goals of the Economic Crime Project have been (1) to enhance the effectiveness of local economic crime prosecution and (2) to increase the responsiveness of local criminal justice agencies to community needs. To facilitate translating these general goals into concrete activities, the ECP (National District Attorneys Association, 1974) provided local units with the following set of guidelines:

(1) Repair swindles and merchandising swindles were given top priority. Optional priorities included the energy crisis (contrived shortages), health, medical, and welfare frauds, and housing, real estate, construction, and land frauds.

(2) Local units were encouraged to "do the 'doable' and seek redress for the most flagrant and pervasive *local* economic crime offenses no matter how modest those offenses might be."

(3) Felony prosecutions were to be sought wherever possible.

(4) Cases involving multiple offenders or multiple victims (major impact cases) also were given high priority.

(5) Units were encouraged to prosecute the easiest cases first to achieve quick results.

(6) Cases involving disadvantaged victims (the elderly, poor, and minorities) were to receive special attention, since these were the people least capable of protecting themselves and most likely to be injured by economic crime.

BACKGROUND OF THE ECU

The ECU in which the present study was conducted was established in 1973 as one of the 15 original pilot programs of the Economic Crime Project. It was part of the criminal division within a county prosecutor's office in a Great Lakes state. The metropolitan population of the county, which covered 500 square miles, was approaching one million at the time of the study in 1979.

The prosecutor's office was staffed by 45 attorneys, 9 investigators, 43 secretarial, clerical, and administrative personnel, and 6 legal interns. The ECU was composed of three full-time attorneys, one full-time investigator, and one part-time legal intern. The unit had investigated over 1000 cases during the first six years of its existence. Two-thirds of these cases were closed administratively without prosecution, and one-third were prosecuted as criminal cases. The types of offenses investigated and prosecuted by the unit included embezzlement, business opportunity fraud, public corruption and bribery, insurance fraud, securities fraud, and welfare fraud.

METHODOLOGY

Fifteen to twenty hours per week over a six-month period were spent in the prosecutor's office collecting four types of data: descriptive information from a stratified random sample of cases closed between 1973 and 1978, copies of 1979 monthly case reports, observations of ECU procedures and activities, and interviews with key ECU personnel.[3] Additional materials pertinent to Economic Crime Project goals were obtained from U.S. government publications, from ECP newsletters and brochures, and from the official journal of the National District Attorneys Association, *The Prosecutor*. In the remainder of this chapter these data will be analyzed to assess how closely this particular ECU adhered to national project guidelines in performing its tasks.

ADHERENCE TO NATIONAL PROJECT GUIDELINES

The assessment of the ECU's adherence to national project guidelines was made in two ways. First, the guidelines were compared against a set of criteria which the ECU staff used in screening potential cases. Second, the national guidelines were compared against the types of cases actually accepted for investigation and prosecution by the unit.

ECU Staff Case Screening Criteria

Unlike other prosecutorial units, the ECU generally did not receive cases which were already investigated by some other law enforcement agency, such as a local police department. Instead, the ECU prosecutors were similar to the federal white-collar crime prosecutors studied by Katz (1979); they conducted most of their own investigations with the aid of a full-time investigator. Local police departments were generally either unable or unwilling to devote resources to investigating "paper crimes" which were not considered the equivalent of such "real crimes" as murder, rape, robbery, and the other index crimes. Because of police reluctance to investigate economic crimes, the ECU was often contacted directly by victims who had been referred to the ECU by police or another agency (e.g., the Better Business Bureau) which could not or would not handle the case.

Based on observations and interviews with ECU staff members, six criteria were identified as key factors in the decision to accept a potential case for investigation:

(1) *The activities involved constituted an apparent felony.* The county prosecutor's office was required to handle felony cases that occurred within its jurisdiction but could dispose of misdeameanors by transferring them to a municipal attorney's office. The ECU staff said they generally followed this policy, although they occasionally accepted cases that did not appear to merit a felony charge if they met one or more of the remaining criteria.

(2) *The case involved multiple victims.* The staff believed that multiple-victim cases were generally more serious than single-victim cases, primarily because the loss involved was likely to be greater. The existence of multiple victims also was seen as an indication that the illegal activity was intentional rather than an error in judgment or a misunderstanding.

(3) *The illegal activity appeared to be widespread within the local community.* The ECU maintained close ties with a network of agencies interested in controlling economic crime (e.g., the state securities division, the Better Business Bureau). When it became apparent to one or more of these agencies that a particular type of scheme had become prevalent, the ECU targeted it for immediate action. Even if no prosecution developed, the staff believed that an investigation alone was often enough to discourage the perpetrators from continuing their operation.

(4) *The case involved some degree of complexity or difficulty.* The ECU staff preferred to tackle only the most difficult or complex cases, leaving the simpler ones to the regular criminal division staff whenever possible. They argued that their time should be reserved for those cases in which their special expertise was needed.

(5) *The case involved "big money."* The staff said they preferred to handle cases involving losses of at least $10,000. The greater the monetary loss, the more serious the case was presumed to be. In addition, large loss cases were likely to attract the attention of the media, and the staff enjoyed projecting a public image of carrying on important work.

(6) *The ECU's caseload would permit the addition of another case.* The consensus was that the unit could handle approximately 40 open cases at any one time, given existing resources and personnel. While there was always room for a serious or complex case, the staff felt that too many cases could stretch their limited resources so thin that effectiveness would be impeded.

The first three criteria—felonies, multiple victims, and prevalence of the activity—coincide with several of the guidelines set down by the national Economic Crime Project. The last three criteria—complexity, dollar amount of loss, and current caseload—do not correspond with national project guidelines. In fact, instead of prosecuting the easiest cases, the staff said this ECU went after the most complex or difficult cases. It should be noted that the ECP's advice to take the easiest cases first was given when the project was just beginning. This particular ECU had six years' experience by the time of the present study. The staff probably believed they had the expertise to go after the more complex cases by that time. Two additional national guidelines were not mentioned at all by ECU staff members: One was the top-priority emphasis on repair and merchandising swindles; the other was the emphasis on cases involving disadvantaged victims. Overall, the staff presented the ECU's mission as investigation and prosecution of the most serious and prevalent economic crimes within the community. The type of offense and the victim's status were apparently of minor significance compared with the scope of the crime and its impact on the community.

Once a case was investigated by the ECU, the decision to prosecute or not prosecute the case depended on whether the staff believed they could prove the defendant's guilt in court. Staff members contended that they would seek an indictment only if they believed they could win the case in court if they had to. Thus, the major criterion for prosecuting an economic crime case was its apparent provability—an assessment of whether a judge and/or jury could be convinced of the defendant's guilt.

Factors that influenced the assessment of provability were less tangible and therefore more difficult to categorize than factors influencing the decision to investigate a case. One significant factor was the credibility of the witnesses' (generally the victims') testimony. Another important element was the quality of the paper evidence—how easy or difficult it would be to document the illegal financial manipulations or to trace the money back to the defendant's hands. The ECU staff's assessment of the case along these two dimensions was a crucial part of the decision process leading either to a prosecution or dropping the case. Thus, once a case was accepted for investigation by the ECU, the strength of the evidence, both documentary and testimonial, became the central factor in the decision to prosecute.

Characteristics of ECU Cases

Closed case files contained valuable information about the kinds of cases processed by the ECU. Analysis of these case files along several dimensions reveals patterns in the types of cases selected for investigation and prosecution over the period 1973-1978. In addition, monthly reports for 1979 indicate whether any changes were occurring in the types of cases being selected by the unit at the time of this study. By comparing these data with national project guidelines, it is possible to determine whether ECU procedures promoted selection of the types of cases suggested by the national project. Furthermore, it is possible to assess the extent to which the staff fulfilled the unit's own criteria for case acceptance.

Although available data did not indicate the prevalence of economic crimes within the community, they did provide information on six pertinent dimensions: number of victims, types of offense, type of victim, race of suspect, gender of suspect, and dollar amount of loss. The data on each dimension will be presented for all cases investigated by the unit and for that subset of cases selected for prosecution.

Between 1973 and 1978 approximately three-fourths of the cases deemed prosecutable by the ECU involved only one victim.[4] This is probably a consequence of the fact that nearly three-fourths of all cases investigated by the unit also involved only one victim. Thus, it appears that the ECU did not adhere very closely to the multiple-victim criterion in selecting cases for investigation or prosecution. The 1979 monthly report data do indicate a change in this pattern, however. Multiple-victim cases comprised over half (54 percent) of the prosecutable cases that year, while single-victim cases dropped to just 38 percent of the total. (The number of victims was unknown for 8 percent of the prosecutable cases.)

As Table 3.1 indicates, between 1973 and 1978 over 90 percent of the cases deemed prosecutable by the ECU involved only two general categories of crime: (1) fraud against government, public agencies, or utilities and (2) corruption, abuse of trust, or theft. Nearly all cases of fraud against government, public agencies, or utilities were welfare recipient frauds. Thus, the single offense most often investigated and prosecuted by the ECU during its first six years was welfare fraud. In the second leading offense category—corruption, abuse of trust, or theft—most of the cases were embezzlements. Sales fraud and repair fraud, the two top-priority

TABLE 3.1   Percentage Distribution of Cases by Type of Offense

Type of Offense[a]	1973-1978 Case Files		1979 Monthly Reports	
	All Cases	Prosecutable Cases	All Cases	Prosecutable Cases
Investments	7	3	11	4
Financing, credit, banking	3	4	11	11
Corruption, abuse of trust, theft	18	28	39	50
Fraud against government, public agencies, utilities	43	63	11	8
Trade practices	1	0	3	0
Housing, land, real estate, construction	4	0	6	8
Sales and repairs	15	2	0	0
Insurance	0	0	9	11
Health, medical care	0	0	2	0
Other	6	0	6	8
Unknown	3	0	2	0
Total	100	100	100	100
(N)	(207)	(98)	(109)	(26)

[a] Offense categories are based on those used by the Economic Crime Project.

offenses according to national project guidelines, received little, if any, attention from the ECU. These two types of offenses together comprised only two percent of prosecutable cases from 1973 to 1978.

The ECU phased out welfare fraud investigations and prosecutions in late 1978 when a separate Welfare Fraud Unit was established in the prosecutor's office. The ECU's monthly reports for 1979 reflect this shift in focus. With the elimination of welfare fraud cases, frauds against government, public agencies, or utilities decreased from 43 percent to only 11 percent of the unit's total case volume, and cases involving corruption, abuse of trust, or theft increased from 18 percent to 39 percent of the unit's overall caseload. The latter offenses comprised fully half of the

TABLE 3.2   Percentage Distribution of Cases by Type of Victim

Type of Victim	1973-1978 Case Files		1979 Monthly Reports	
	All Cases	Prosecutable Cases	All Cases	Prosecutable Cases
Individual	31	4	30	23
Private orga- nization	13	17	32	46
Government agen- cy or state	51	77	20	12
Combination	2	2	12	15
Unknown	3	0	6	4
Total	100	100	100	100
(N)	(207)	(98)	(109)	(26)

ECU's prosecutable cases in 1979. Sales and repair frauds also disappeared from the ECU's caseload in 1979, but the unit seemed to be branching out in other areas with the addition of insurance frauds and health and medical care frauds.

In slightly more than half (51 percent) of the 1973-1978 cases, the victim was a government agency or the state (Table 3.2). This is not a surprising finding in view of the large number of frauds against the state welfare department processed by the ECU. When prosecutable cases alone were examined, the percentage of cases involving a state agency as the victim increased from 51 percent to 77 percent, while the percentage involving a private citizen as the victim decreased from 31 percent to just 4 percent. Thus, the ECU apparently favored public agencies over private individuals as victims in economic crime cases.

As Table 3.2 indicates, after welfare fraud cases were eliminated, the proportion of investigations and prosecutions on behalf of public agency victims declined rather sharply. During 1979, only 20 percent of the victims in all cases could be classified as government agencies or the state. Although private individuals did come to comprise a larger percentage of the victims in prosecutable cases during 1979, it should be noted that private organizations represented almost half the victims. Private organizations, therefore, made up for part of the decline in public agency victims.

Thus, it does not appear that the ECU was actively involved in protecting the interests of private citizens. The majority of victims were public and private organizations rather than individuals. In addition, the high percentage of welfare fraud cases investigated by the ECU suggests that the unit may have devoted more attention to members of disadvantaged groups as suspects rather than as victims in economic crime cases. An examination of two suspect characteristics provides additional evidence of this tendency.

According to the case files, the vast majority (71 percent) of suspects investigated by the ECU between 1973 and 1978 were individuals. An additional 8 percent were individuals who conducted business as organizations, such as self-employed sales and repair persons or contractors.[5] The remaining suspects were organizations or combinations of individuals and organizations.

As Table 3.3 indicates, the suspect's race could not be determined for almost half (45 percent) of the case file sample.[6] However, among those cases for which the information was available, 60 percent of the suspects were nonwhite. Blacks comprised nearly half the ECU's suspects in prosecutable cases. This can be attributed largely to the fact that blacks represented approximately 80 percent of the suspects in welfare fraud cases.

The distribution of cases on the variable of suspect gender is also presented in Table 3.3. Females were suspects in almost two-thirds of the cases deemed prosecutable by the ECU. This is an unusual finding, since females traditionally have represented only a small percentage of suspects in criminal cases. However, the high percentage of female suspects is consistent with the fact that the vast majority (92 percent) of welfare fraud cases involved female suspects.

As previous data have suggested, the ECU did not have a history of favoring disadvantaged victims. Moreover, to the extent that women and blacks—especially women and blacks on welfare—are members of disadvantaged groups, the ECU had a history of prosecuting such persons rather than protecting them. By emphasizing welfare fraud cases for six years, the unit completely inverted one of the major guidelines of the national Economic Crime Project—devoting special attention to cases involving disadvantaged victims. Before addressing the question of why this pattern may have developed within the ECU, it is instructive to examine case file data on one final dimension.

Although national project guidelines suggested no minimum dollar limit for case acceptability, the ECU staff indicated that they preferred cases involving substantial losses of $10,000 and above. While there were no data on this variable in the 1979 monthly reports, the sample of case files

TABLE 3.3 Percentage Distribution of Cases by Suspect Race and Gender

1973-1978 Case Files

Race	All Cases	Prosecutable Cases	Gender	All Cases	Prosecutable Cases
Black	31	48	Female	51	63
White	20	30	Male	39	33
Native American	1	1	Female/male co-suspects	2	3
Individual/ organizational co-suspects	3	1	Individual/organi- zational co-suspects	3	1
Unknown	45	20	Unknown	5	0
Total	100%	100%	Total	100%[a]	100%
(N)	(166)[a]	(98)	(N)	(166)[a]	(98)

[a] The remaining 41 cases involved only organizational suspects.

indicated that the $10,000 minimum had not been strictly applied. The ECU prosecuted few cases involving more than $10,000 in losses (19 percent of prosecutable cases). In fact, the majority (61 percent) of cases deemed prosecutable by the unit involved losses under $5,000. The ECU was generally successful in restricting its focus to felony cases. This was indicated by the fact that only 4 percent of the cases fell below the felony minimum of $150. However, the amount of loss in most cases did not even come close to the $10,000 mark the staff claimed was their lower limit for acceptability. The ECU did not legally have the privilege of refusing to accept cases simply because there not enough money involved. Nevertheless, the unit did not investigate and prosecute "big money" cases on a regular basis. Instead, its efforts were concentrated on crimes involving losses smaller than the average bank robbery.[7] In relative terms the ECU was prosecuting the "small fry" of economic crime rather than the major offenders.

DISCUSSION AND CONCLUSION

The ECU did not adhere very closely to either the guidelines established by the national Economic Crime Project or the criteria for case acceptability stated by its own staff. The unit did not give top priority to repair and merchandising swindles, did not emphasize cases involving multiple victims, and did not give special attention to cases involving disadvantaged victims.

In addition, the ECU did not investigate or prosecute "big money" cases, but spent most of its time going after small-time welfare cheaters, most of whom were members of disadvantaged groups—the poor, blacks, and women. Such cases generally did not fit the staff's criterion of maximum complexity or difficulty. Much of the investigative work had already been accomplished by the state welfare department. Welfare frauds involved two relatively straightforward types of illegal actions. In one type of case the recipient falsely claimed to have lost his or her monthly welfare check and received a replacement. The crime was discovered when the welfare department received two cancelled checks, both the "lost" check and its replacement, bearing identical signatures. In the other type of fraud the recipient failed to notify the welfare department after obtaining employment or falsely claimed to be unemployed on his or her reassessment forms. Since many of those who did find employment were hired by state agencies under CETA programs, these crimes were discovered through a computer match-up of social security numbers on welfare rolls with those on the state payroll. In most cases, the difficult task was locating and apprehending the suspect, not proving his or her guilt. Even ECU staff members downplayed the difficulty and the degree of challenge involved in welfare fraud cases. Thus, there is evidence that the ECU did not adhere to the criterion of selecting the most complex or difficult cases for investigation and prosecution.

Since welfare fraud cases were easy and straightforward prosecutions, the ECU did adhere to the national guideline of prosecuting the easiest cases first. However, it continued to prosecute the easiest cases for six years. Moreover, by concentrating so heavily on welfare frauds, the ECU failed to give special attention to disadvantaged victims and instead gave that special attention to disadvantaged suspects—poor blacks and women on welfare. The question is, why did the unit devote so much attention to this type of crime when other offenses might have coincided more closely with national project goals and guidelines?

The answer to the question involves several interrelated factors. One is that the welfare frauds were indeed economic crimes, well within the scope of the ECU's responsibility and enforcement authority. The unit was presented with packages of evidence from the welfare department. Since the crimes occurred within the ECU's jurisdiction, the staff had very little choice but to accept them. Given the large number of welfare cases received and the small size of the ECU, there was not much time left over to handle other types of cases.

Another factor is that the emphasis on welfare fraud cases allowed the ECU to accomplish an important immediate goal within the prosecutor's office: gaining convictions. This prosecutor's office was similar to most others in that high conviction rates were stressed as measures of successful job performance. As a number of other researchers have noted, chief prosecutors, who are generally elected officials, depend on conviction statistics in order to maintain themselves in office (Alschuler, 1968; Neubauer, 1974; Reiss, 1975).

The prosecutor's office that sponsored this ECU was certainly typical in this respect. Each unit and each attorney within each unit was encouraged to win cases both in and out of court. Guilty pleas were just as good as guilty verdicts. The pressure to win was keenly felt by the ECU staff. They took pride in their overall conviction record of 88 percent, and they frequently stated that their superiors placed a great deal of emphasis on securing convictions. In fact, in their more cynical moments, staff members suggested that winning cases was even more important than determining a defendant's guilt or innocence.

Welfare fraud cases represented relatively quick and easy convictions. Most involved instances of false statements by welfare recipients who said that they had lost their checks or that they were currently unemployed. Proving that these statements were fraudulent involved simply compiling evidence from welfare department records, state payroll records, handwriting analyses, and Regiscope photographs.[8] Most of this material was collected by the welfare department before the cases were even sent to the ECU. Thus, these cases could be disposed of with relative ease by the staff. In addition, many of the suspects in welfare fraud cases were indeed indigent and therefore required the services of public defenders. Securing guilty pleas or verdicts against the clients of public defenders required less effort and preparation than going up against high-priced private legal talent retained by white-collar or elite criminals. For these reasons, welfare fraud cases represented a quick and easy way of enhancing a major goal of the prosecutor's office: to secure convictions and maintain a winning record.

In sum, the one national project guideline this ECU appeared to fulfill better than any other was doing the "doable." This directive most closely conformed to the day-to-day constraints and exigencies under which the unit operated within the prosecutor's office.

In view of the findings of this research, designers of national crime control programs should consider the organization and operation of the local agencies that will implement those programs. Policy makers should recognize that national program directives that conflict with local agency objectives may be selectively transformed into guidelines that more nearly fit preexisting arrangements. While this may not always produce negative consequences, it can lead to situations in which the agency succeeds in accomplishing some goals to the detriment of others. In this case, by doing the "doable" and seeking to gain convictions, the ECU inverted one of the guidelines of the Economic Crime Project and directed efforts at members of disadvantaged groups as perpetrators rather than victims of economic crime.

NOTES

1. The 15 original ECUs in the Project were Los Angeles County, Sacramento County, San Diego County (California); Miami/Dade County (Florida); Wichita/Sedgwick County (Kansas); Baltimore City (Maryland); Flint/Genesee County (Michigan); Omaha/Douglas County (Nebraska); Brooklyn/Kings County, Buffalo/Erie County, Mineola/Nassau County (New York); Columbus/Franklin County (Ohio);

Houston/Harris County (Texas); Burlington/Chittenden County (Vermont) and Seattle/King County (Washington).

2. These agencies include the U.S. Postal Inspection Service, FBI, Federal Trade Commission, Securities and Exchange Commission, Department of Transportation, National Highway Traffic Safety Administration, and Department of Justice.

3. The closed case files were stratified on the basis of whether or not they had been deemed prosecutable by the ECU staff. Using a standard formula for calculating sample size (McCarthy, 1970), a random sample of 100 prosecutable and 178 nonprosecutable cases was selected. Ninety-eight prosecutable case files and 109 nonprosecutable case files were located and examined. According to ECU staff members, many of the missing nonprosecutable case files were welfare fraud cases, and the file contents had been returned to the welfare department after the cases were turned down for prosecution.

4. Prosecutable cases were those the staff decided to prosecute. This set of 98 cases includes 2 cases that were rejected or no-billed by the grand jury and thus were never actually prosecuted. It also includes 18 cases for which indictments were returned, but the suspects were never apprehended.

5. The 1979 monthly report data display a slightly different pattern with a decline in individual suspects to 56 percent of the total and an increase in organizational suspects to 40 percent (9 percent organizational suspects alone and 31 percent organizational suspects with individual co-suspects).

6. Race and gender information was not available in the 1979 monthly case reports.

7. According to FBI statistics during the first half of 1975, the average loss due to bank robbery was $6,500 (McCaghy, 1980: 254).

8. Regiscope photographs are those commonly taken by banks and stores in check cashing transactions.

REFERENCES

ALSCHULER, A. (1968) "The prosecutor's role in plea bargaining." Univ. of Chicago Law Rev. 36: 50-112.

KATZ, J. (1979) "Legality and equality—plea bargaining in the prosecution of white-collar and common crimes." Law and Society Rev. 13: 431-459.

McCAGHY, C. (1980) Crime in American Society. New York: Macmillan.

McCARTHY, P. (1970) Sampling: Elementary Principles. Ithaca: New York State School of Industrial and Labor Relations.

National District Attorneys Association (1974) Economic Crime Project: First Annual Report, 1973-1974. Washington, DC: National District Attorneys Association.

NEUBAUER, D. (1974) Criminal Justice in Middle America. Morristown, NJ: General Learning Press.

REISS, A. (1975) "Public prosecutors and criminal prosecution in the United States of America." Juridical Rev. 20: 1-21.

4

Timothy S. Bynum

Michigan State University

PROSECUTORIAL DISCRETION AND THE IMPLEMENTATION OF A LEGISLATIVE MANDATE

Traditional views of public administration as well as "classical" approaches to policy implementation employ a dichotomous conception of the operationalization of administrative directives. That is, prescribed policies and programs are either implemented as planners and administrators envisioned or, through some act of administrative defiance, they are not. While such a simplistic conception undoubtedly contains an element of truth, programs and directives are indeed either implemented or they are not; subsequent studies of implementation have emphasized a range of factors associated with the degree to which such "orders" are carried out. One of the major factors influencing policy implementation has, somewhat obviously, been found to be the degree to which the principal actors are interested, committed, and supportive of the concepts represented by the policy or program (McLaughlin, 1976; Van Meter and Van Horn, 1975). The greater the commitment of those carrying out the implementation, the more likely the implementation is to be successful. Second, the degree of clarity of the policy directives has been found to strongly influence the manner in which policies and programs are implemented (Radin, 1977). The attempt to implement ambiguous policies displaces the interpretation of policy intent from administrators to line workers carrying out the policy. Rein and Rabinovitz (1978) note that when such legislative directives are implemented, lower-level practitioners resolve this dilemma through their normal decision-making processes and interpret the meaning of the policy in the context of their routine activities. Recent studies have thus rejected the traditional static view of the implementation process in favor of a much more dynamic one. In fact, Bardach (1977) presents this process as a series of "games" involving interpretation, negotiation, and exchange through which policy directives are operationalized. However, even in situations where environmental conditions are "ripe" for policy implementation—that is, directives are clearly stated and widely supported by implementors—there may continue to be a great deal of variation in the manner in which such policies are carried out. The present study is an investigation of such variation in the implementation of a legislatively mandated sentencing provision.

In 1976, in the wake of public concern about street crime, the Michigan legislature enacted a statute prescribing a two-year mandatory prison sentence for individuals who were in possession of a firearm during the commission of a felony. This statute, which took effect January 1, 1977, contained extremely "tough" provisions to add to the prosecutor's tools with which to fight crime: The two-year sentence was to be served consecutively and prior to any additional sentence imposed, and no probation, suspended sentence, or parole was to be allowed for those convicted of this offense. Thus, the new "gun law" was not only politically popular with the "get tough with crime" public, but also a number of highly influential prosecutors were very supportive as well as instrumental in getting the legislation passed. In addition to receiving wide political support, the legislation was quite specific in its directives as to whom the legislation was intended to apply and the manner of sanction that was to be imposed. In fact, the legislative authors went to great lengths to specify clearly that neither judicial (prohibition of probation) nor administrative (prohibition of parole) discretion would be permitted to mitigate the application of this mandatory sanction. Thus, a situation was created in which the policy to be implemented was clearly stated and had a high degree of not only public but agency support as well. Although judicial and administrative discretion was addressed in the legislation, prosecutorial discretion was not. In spite of these ideal implementation conditions, previous research on prosecutorial decision making leads me to hypothesize that there will be substantial variation in the implementation of this statute.

A number of environmental pressures, in addition to the prosecutor's own predilections, serve to shape prosecutorial policies and decisions (Mellon et al., 1981). These environmental influences come both from within the criminal justice community as well as from the prosecutor's political constituency. Within the criminal justice environment the prosecutor is under a great deal of pressure to have a high conviction percentage in order to appear effective and efficient for funding considerations. In addition, prosecutors are beseiged by police to issue warrants in cases they want prosecuted, by sheriffs to not overload the jail with pretrial detainees, and by judges to clear the court calendar. Since the prosecutors need positive relationships with other criminal justice actors (including the defense attorney), a system of exchange relationships develops which affects prosecutorial decision making (Cole, 1970; Skolnick, 1967).

Prosecutorial policies and decisions are also influenced by public and political influences in the external environment. If a particularly heinous crime occurs or public concern increases about a particular type of criminal behavior (e.g., rape, child abuse, armed robbery), the prosecutor feels constrained to pursue prosecution vigorously in these types of cases. Since prosecutors are elected officials and many have further political aspirations, they are particularly sensitive to public sentiment about crime.

Thus, the prosecutor faces the dilemma of having to appear publicly "tough on crime" while responding to organizational pressure to dispose of cases quickly and efficiently. Traditionally, this dilemma has been resolved through plea bargaining (Newman, 1966; Rosett and Cressey, 1976). However, many new sentencing proposals emphasizing mandatory penalties, as well as court-watching groups, have made the charging decision much more crucial to the determination of criminal penalties. Rather than bargaining for a particular sentence, the prosecutor may be more likely to exercise discretion in the charging decision.

A recent study of the charging practice of different prosecutors identified four types of criteria on which the decision to prosecute is made (Mellon et al., 1981; Jacoby et al., 1979). Some prosecutor's offices screen cases on the basis of the legal sufficiency of the case (i.e., Does the evidence presented in the police report substantiate the crime charged?). Other prosecutors emphasize trial sufficiency (i.e., If the case goes to trial, will it be won?). A third group of prosecutors operate according to a system efficiency model which emphasizes the early disposition of a large volume of cases. A fourth group makes decisions according to a defendant rehabilitation model, in which the prosecutor actively diverts a large number of minor or first offenders and vigorously prosecutes repeat offenders.

Although these legal styles are instructive in describing overall prosecutorial policies, they do not indicate the specific criteria on which the charging decision is made. Additional studies on the charging decisions have indicated that local politics and defendant social characteristics are likely to influence prosecution (Jacob, 1963; Sudnow, 1965). The decision to prosecute is an administrative decision and open to little review and public scrutiny. Green (1964) has suggested that if discrimination exists within the administration of justice, it most likely occurs in these decisions characterized by low visibility. Subsequent research on a number of low-visibility decisions has found the existence of racial disparity in the decision to arrest (Piliavin and Briar, 1964) as well as the decision to grant conditional release from incarceration (Peterson and Friday, 1975; Bynum, 1981). The prosecutorial decision is similarly a low-visibility decision subject to internal and external environmental pressures. These environmental pressures have been shown to affect policy implementation in general (Nakamura and Smallwood, 1980) as well as influence specific prosecutorial decisions (Jacob, 1963). The present study will focus on the implementation of the Michigan Felony Firearm Statute and the patterns of use of this mandatory sentencing provision.

DATA AND METHOD

The data for this analysis come from the Michigan Felony Sentencing Project. This project was a study of statewide sentencing practices undertaken for the purpose of designing sentencing guidelines for the state of Michigan (Zalman et al., 1979). Data were collected on a stratified (on the basis of type of crime and geographic location) random sample of cases that were disposed of during 1977 in each felony court jurisdiction in the state. Since the gun law did not take effect until January 1, 1977, cases in which the offense occurred prior to that date were excluded from the analysis. The sample was selected from the Criminal Case Conviction Register, which is submitted by probation officers to the state Department of Corrections on all felony convictions, and information was collected from the presentence investigation report.

The analysis was conducted on those robbery cases that were committed after January 1, 1977 and involved the use of a firearm and thus were eligible for prosecution under the felony firearm statute. It is important to note that the sample selection for this chapter was based not on legal category but on case characteristics. This manner of selection maximizes the area of prosecutorial discretion. That is, until the charge of armed robbery has been filed, the prosecutor may not feel public and organizational constraints to file the additional gun law charge.

FINDINGS

By applying the sampling procedure, 426 cases were identified that were eligible for prosecution under the felony firearm statute. In contrast to the expectation of full or close to full implementation, only 65 percent of the eligible cases were charged with the gun law. One of the factors that may explain this deviation from the legislative mandate is the differential support for this provision among prosecutors' offices. Table 4.1 presents a breakdown of the state total by court jurisdiction.From these data we note substantial variation between counties in the use of the gun law. Courts A, B, and C represent the Detroit metropolitan area and are the three largest courts in the state. In these courts 70 percent of the eligible cases were charged with the gun law. However, in 19 of the remaining 21 jurisdictions the gun law was used in either all or none of the cases, and in one of the other two jurisdictions a similar trend was noted with 90 percent of eligible cases being charged with the gun law. Since in most of these courts there were very few eligible cases, one should be cautious in the interpretation of these results; however, in the nonmetropolitan area there do appear to be implicit, if not explicit, prosecutorial policies concerning the use or nonuse of the felony firearm statute.

Thus, a large proportion of the variation in the application of the gun law in the nonmetropolitan counties may be explained as a result of jurisdictional differences. In the metropolitan counties, however, there appears to be, within jurisdiction, substantial variation in the prosecution of eligible cases under the gun law. The remainder of this analysis will focus on the manner in which the defendant's legal and social character-istics differentiate between cases selected for prosecution and those not subjected to this additional sanction within the metropolitan area.

Table 4.2 presents the results of an analysis of the gun law decision by the defendant's age, race, and prior felony convictions. These data indicate that blacks were significantly more likely ($p < .01$) to receive the gun law charge than were whites. Seventy-four percent of black defendants com-pared to 56 percent of white defendants faced additional felony firearm charges. The gamma and chi-square values indicate a strong and significant relationship between these variables.

A dramatic difference was also observed with respect to the defendant's prior felony record. While there was a statistically significant positive relationship ($p < .001$) between prior felony convictions and being charged with the gun law, this observation appears to be primarily a result

TABLE 4.1   Use of Gun Law in Robbery Cases by Court Jurisdiction (row percentages in parentheses)

Court	Gun Law Charge	No Gun Law Charge	Total Cases
A	149 (68)	70 (32)	219
B	28 (76)	9 (24)	37
C	52 (75)	17 (25)	69
D	0 (00)	2 (100)	2
E	0 (00)	11 (100)	11
F	2 (100)	0 (00)	2
G	19 (90)	2 (10)	21
H	6 (100)	0 (00)	6
I	0 (00)	4 (100)	4
J	3 (100)	0 (00)	3
K	9 (100)	0 (00)	9
L	4 (22)	14 (78)	18
M	2 (100)	0 (00)	2
N	0 (00)	6 (100)	6
O	0 (00)	2 (100)	2
P	1 (100)	0 (100)	1
Q	0 (00)	3 (100)	3
R	0 (00)	2 (100)	2
S	0 (00)	1 (100)	1
T	0 (00)	1 (100)	1
U	1 (100)	0 (00)	1
V	0 (00)	1 (100)	1
W	0 (00)	3 (100)	3
X	0 (00)	2 (100)	2
Total	276 (65)	150 (35)	426

of the manner in which defendants with three or more such convictions were treated. While 65 percent of those defendants having no convictions were charged with the gun law and 66 percent of those with one or two such convictions were charged with the gun law, 88 percent of defendants with three or more convictions were charged.

TABLE 4.2   Use of Gun Law by Race, Age, and Prior Felony Convictions (row percentages in parentheses)

Variable	x^2	Gamma	Gun Law Charge	No Gun Law Charge	Total
Race	8.75**	.38			
White			41 (56)	32 (44)	73
Black			184 (74)	64 (26)	248
Priors	13.40***	.20			
None			89 (65)	47 (35)	136
1 or 2			76 (66)	40 (34)	116
3 or more			64 (88)	9 (12)	73
Age	5.38*	.27			
22 and under			99 (64)	56 (36)	155
Over 22			125 (76)	40 (24)	165
Total			229 (70)	96 (30)	325

*p<.05
**p<.01
***p<.001

A significant relationship (p < .05) was also observed between the age of the defendant and the charging with the gun law. Younger offenders were seen to have a slight advantage, as 64 percent of those 22 and younger were charged with the gun law compared to 76 percent of older defendants.

Although these bivariate relationships are interesting and instructive, the impact of these variables may be confounded by the variable intercorrelations. Thus, a multivariate analysis is in order. Because traditional approaches of multiple regression and analysis of variance are not appropriate in situations for analysis of models having a dichotomous dependent variable (Palmer and Carlson, 1976; Hanushek and Jackson, 1977; Swafford, 1980), a logistic regression (logit) model was adopted to determine the unique contributions of these independent variables. Table 4.3 presents the results of a logit analysis. This nonlinear solution involves fitting a logistic function to the data in which the dependent variable is the natural logarithm of the odds of getting the gun law. The coefficients derived through this method indicate the addition each independent variable (and interactions of these variables) makes to the odds of getting the gun law. While the interpretation of these coefficients is somewhat obscure, another property of the logitistic model allows for a more straightforward interpretation. If the antilog of both sides of the equation is taken, the model becomes multiplicative rather than additive. Since the program employed in this analysis (BMDP Stepwise Logistic Regression) uses only variables that are effect coded, an additional transformation is helpful in the interpretation of these findings. (See Swafford, 1980, for a particularly helpful discussion of the interpretation of findings from logit analysis.)

Focusing on the main effects model in Table 4.3, we note that the prediction of the log-odds (or logit) is given by the equation $\ln (\Omega) = .765 + .472$ RACE $+ .794$ PRIORS1 $- .501$ PRIORS2 $+ .138$ AGE. In the effect coding used, if the defendant was black, a 1 was assigned for race; if white, the value for race was -1. Two design variables were used for prior felony convictions to describe the three categories of this variable; for defendants having no prior conviction, PRIOR1 was coded -1 and PRIOR2 was coded -1. For those having 1 or 2 prior convictions, PRIOR1 was coded 0 and PRIOR2 was coded 1. The category of 3 or more prior convictions was represented by 1 and 0 on the variables PRIOR1 and PRIOR2, respectively. Those over 22 were represented by 1 and those 22 and under were coded -1 on the age variable. Thus, for a defendant who was black, had three prior convictions, and was over 22, the logit of his receiving the gun

TABLE 4.3 Logit Analysis of the Effect of Age, Race, and Prior Offenses on the Use of the Gun Law

Parameter	Main Effects Model		First-Order Model		Saturated Model	
	b	x^2	*b*	x^2	*b*	x^2
Constant	.756	—	2.251	—	1.790	—
Race	.472	10.22***	.578	9.73**	1.232	.00
Priors		10.65**		12.11*		16.17***
(1)	.794		3.576		4.428	
(2)	-.501		-1.793		-2.985	
Age	.138	1.07	-1.458	2.65	-2.182	6.02*
Age*Race	—	—	.132	.58	.674	.00
Priors*Race	—	—		1.97		.85
(1)			.354		-.135	
(2)			-.370		.729	
Priors*Age	—	—		7.02*		12.04**
(1)			-3.304		-2.972	
(2)			1.638		.437	
Age*Priors*Race	—	—	—	—		13.32**
(1)					-.707	
(2)					1.654	
Goodness of Fit	24.331***		13.323***		.006	

*p < .05
**p < .01
***p < .001

law would be .756 + .472 (1) + .794 (1) − .501 (0) + .138 (1) = 2.16. The antilog of this estimate (8.67) is the predicted odds of the defendant getting the gun law. Thus, an individual falling into this category has an estimated 90 percent chance of getting the gun law. Conversely, a defendant who is white, has no prior convictions, and is under 22 has but a 46 percent chance to be charged with the gun law.

The coefficients in the main effects model also note the unique contribution of each of the independent variables. The race and priors variables remain highly significant when controls were introduced through this procedure. That is, even controlling for prior offenses, black defendants were significantly ($p < .001$) more likely to have to face additional gun law charges. The antilog of the magnitude of the difference between the coefficients for blacks and whites (the value that would have been obtained if dummy coding were used) gives a straightforward interpretation of this effect (Swafford, 1980). From this procedure, we note that controlling for age and prior felony convictions, blacks were 2.6 (antilog of .944) times as likely to be charged with the gun law as whites. Similarily controlling for race and age, defendants having three or more prior convictions were three times as likely to get the gun law as those having less than three convictions.

The significance of the goodness of fit chi-square indicates the existence of higher-order effects that are contributing to the observed distribution of the data. In the model containing only the first-order effects, the coefficients for race and priors continue to be significant, while the interaction effect of age and priors emerges as significant. However, the goodness of fit statistic still indicates that this model does not adequately fit the data. Thus, there is no more parsimonious model than the saturated model that provides a satisfactory fit to these observations as long as the hierarchical rule is maintained. This situation is due to the significance of the interaction term of all three independent variables in the full model.

The significance of this interaction term, coupled with the loss of significance of the main effect of race, indicates that the impact of race on use of the gun law is primarily through its relationship with prior convictions and age. One possible interpretation of such a finding is that race is important in certain categories of age and prior offenses. That is, since almost everyone with three or more prior felony convictions is charged with the gun law, little racial discrimination exists within this category. However, among those with fewer prior offenses, 35 percent do not get the gun law. In this group, we might expect blacks to be more likely than whites to face additional gun law charges.

DISCUSSION

Recent studies of the policy implementation process have emphsized two important factors in the determination of successful implementation: clarity of policy directives and commitment of implementors. The Michigan felony firearm statute provides an example of a legislative policy directive that was both clearly stated and well supported by the public as well as by prosecutors who would be responsible for its implementation. Such a situation would lead one to believe that an extremely high percentage of eligible defendants would be prosecuted under this statute. Yet only 65 percent of such cases statewide were charged with the gun law. Furthermore, in nonmetropolitan jurisdictions, the gun law tended to be used on all cases or none. Although the sample of these cases is small, such a finding implies the existence of certain jurisdiction-specific characteristics (e.g., public sentiment, prosecutorial preferences, date of next prosecutorial election) which determine the implementation or nonimplementation of the mandatory sentencing provision. However, within the metropolitan courts there was also substantial variation in the application of the gun law to eligible defendants.

In an earlier study of the use of the gun law in one of the metropolitan Detroit courts, Heumann and Loftin (1979) note the prosecutor's firm public stance and support for mandatory sentencing of these offenders. Not only did the prosecutor make numerous public statements concerning his support for the felony firearm statute, but he forbade his assistants from bargaining on this charge. Review procedures were instituted and sanctions were imposed on those assistant prosecutors who were not diligent in their prosecution under this statute. Thus, there is no doubt that there was substantial support for and commitment to the gun law in this office. However, even in this urban area where there was a great deal of concern about street crime as well as negative sanctions imposed for prosecutorial noncompliance with the statute, a sizable percentage of eligible defendants were not prosecuted. Earlier studies of prosecutorial decision making have noted the environmental pressures and constraints influencing case decisions (Mellon et al., 1981; Jacob, 1963; Cole, 1970). Various political, economic, workload, and organizational factors shape the prosecutor's operating environment in which bargain and exchange are the rule (Skolnick, 1967; Rosett and Cressey, 1976). Such an environment is not conducive to mandatory rules regardless if they are legislatively prescribed or ordered by the chief prosecutor. Heumann and Loftin (1979) noted the development of adaptive strategies by assistant prosecutors and defense attorneys to circumvent the mandatory aspects of this statute. Selection of judges who opposed the gun law on constitutional grounds, the request for bench trials, and bargaining for a sentence adjustment on the primary offense to compensate for the additional two years were all viewed as methods of managing this mandatory provision. The present study indicates that an additional adaptive strategy involves the decision to bring the gun law charge in the first place.

The fact that there is less than full implementation of this policy begs the question, "Is there any systematic difference between cases prosecuted and those not prosecuted?" The present study also suggests the existence of a racial bias in the selection of defendants for prosecution. Controlling for prior felony convictions, black defendants were more likely to receive the gun law. Although the present research has shown that this difference was not a function of the age or criminal record of the defendant, certain other aspects of the criminal incident (e.g., harm to the victim) may have precipitated this response from the prosecutor. While we cannot rule out the existence of such alternative explanations, we also must acknowledge the apparent discriminatory implementation of the felony firearm statute.

What is indeed clear is the importance of the number of prior felony convictions. It is apparent that prosecutors in the three metropolitan courts used the gun law as a habitual offender statute. That is, the major difference due to the defendant's prior record occurred only after the individual had three prior felony convictions. This pattern of findings suggests that what the prosecutors desired in their advocacy for the gun law was not in fact a mandatory sentence for a specific offense but instead the increased discretion to apply this mandatory provision to a select group of offenders. The findings from this study suggest that the recipients of this charge tended to be black and/or persistent offenders.

REFERENCES

BARDACH, E. (1977) The Implementation Game. Cambridge: MIT Press.
BYNUM, T. S. (1981) "Parole decision making and Native Americans," pp. 75-88 in R. L. McNeely and E. Pope (eds.) Race, Crime, and Criminal Justice. Beverly Hills, CA: Sage.
COLE, G. F. (1970) "The decision to prosecute." Law and Society Rev. 4: 313-343.
GREEN, E. (1964) "Inter- and intra-racial crime relative to sentencing." J. of Criminal Law, Criminology and Police Science 55: 348-358.
HANUSHEK, E. and J. JACKSON (1977) Statistical Methods for Social Scientists. New York: Academic Press.

HEUMANN, M. and C. LOFTIN (1979) "Mandatory sentencing and the abolition of plea bargaining: the Michigan felony firearm statute." Law and Society Rev. 13: 393-430.

JACOB, H. (1963) "Politics and criminal prosecution in New Orleans." Tulane Studies in Pol. Sci. 8: 77-98.

JACOBY, J., E. RATLEDGE, and S. TURNER (1979) Research on Prosecutorial Decision Making. Washington, DC: Government Printing Office.

McLAUGHLIN, M. (1976) "Implementation as mutual adaptation," pp. 167-180 in W. Williams and R. Elmore (eds.) Social Program Implementation. New York: Academic Press.

MELLON, L., J. JACOBY, and M. BREWER (1981) "The prosecutor constrained by his environment: a new look at discretionary justice in the United States." J. of Criminal Law and Criminology 72: 52-81.

NAKAMURA, R. and F. SMALLWOOD (1980) The Politics of Policy Implementation. New York: St. Martin's.

NEWMAN, D. (1966) Conviction: The Determination of Guilt or Innocence Without Trial. Boston: Little, Brown.

PALMER, J. and P. CARLSON (1976) "Problems with the use of regression analysis in prediction studies." J. of Research in Crime and Delinquency 13: 64-81.

PETERSON, D. and P. FRIDAY (1975) "Early release from incarceration: race as a factor in the use of shock probation." J. of Criminal Law and Criminology 66: 79-87.

PILIAVIN, I. and S. BRIAR (1964) "Police encounters with juveniles." Amer. J. of Sociology 70: 206-214.

RADIN, B. (1977) Implementation, Change, and the Federal Bureaucracy. New York: Columbia Univ. Press.

REIN, M. and F. RABINOVITZ (1978) "Implementation: a theoretical perspective," pp. 307-335 in W. Burnham and M. Weinberg (eds.) American Politics and Public Policy. Cambridge: MIT Press.

ROSETT, A. and D. CRESSEY (1976) Justice by Consent: Plea Bargains in the American Courtroom. Philadelphia: Lippincott.

SKOLNICK, J. (1967) "Social control in the adversary system." J. of Conflict Resolution 11: 52-70.

SUDNOW, D. (1965) "Normal crimes: sociological features of the penal code in a public defenders office." Social Problems 12: 255-276.

SWAFFORD, M. (1980) "Three parametric techniques for contingency table analysis: a non-technical commentary." Amer. Soc. Rev. 45: 664-690.

VAN METER, D. and C. VAN HORN (1975) "The policy implementation process: a conceptual framework." Admin. and Society 6: 445-488.

ZALMAN, M., C. OSTROM, P. GUILLIAMS, and G. PEASLEE (1979) Sentencing in Michigan: Report of the Michigan Felony Sentencing Project. Lansing, MI: State Court Administrative Office.

5

Marvin Zalman

Wayne State University

MANDATORY SENTENCING LEGISLATION
Myth and Reality

This chapter reflects on the legislative dynamics of the Michigan mandatory sentencing law known as the felony firearm law. The previous
chapter of this book by Bynum, as well as research by Loftin and
McDowall (1981), show that the legislation had little effect on the certainty or severity of sentences in Detroit, was disregarded by many county
prosecutors, and continues a pattern of discriminatory sentencing. These
implementation studies, which show the law to be flawed, imply that a
rational approach to achieving the goal of gun crime reduction should
begin with a different legislative formulation. This implication reflects a
rationalist bias shared by those writing on the implementation of legislation (Berk et al., 1980; Cook, 1981; Feeley et al., 1977). However, while
legislatures do not set out to act in irrational ways, they often do not
pursue a policy-rational process. In other words, the short- and long-range
goals of legislation, as viewed by the legislature, may and often do include
goals other than the most efficient and effective implementation of the
statute's manifest ends. Furthermore, the way in which the manifest goals
are perceived by the legislature may be quite different from the perception
of implementation analysts.

 In this chapter I suggest that the Michigan Felony Firearm Law is in
part the result of three forces or ways of thinking. The first force is the
political matrix which surrounded the passage of the law. The second is
the peculiar method of assessing facts by legislatures. The third way of
thinking which may have influenced the passage of the felony firearm law

is a discounting device that has led the writer of a law review note to establish a jurisprudential category of "laws that are made to be broken" (Note, 1977).

POLITICAL CONTEXT

The felony firearm law, Public Act No. 6 of 1976, which was approved on February 11, 1976 to take effect on January 1, 1977, was not an isolated instance of legislative concern with penalties. As I noted in 1978, "assessments by those close to the Michigan legislature indicate that concern for sentencing is higher than at any time in the recent past" (Zalman, 1978: 919). The evidence to support this assertion is strong. The sheer number of individual sentencing bills introduced rose from 16 in 1971-1972 to 27 in 1973-1974 to 89 in 1975-1976 and 84 in the 1977 session. The nature of the bills also changed noticeably. In addition to a host of bills aimed at increasing penalties for specific crimes (ranging from driving mopeds on sidewalks to unauthorized possession of atomic bombs!) two kinds of general sentencing laws were introduced. The first included four separate presumptive sentencing bills which sought to overhaul the entire sentencing system (Zalman, 1978: 919-927). The bills were a reflection of a national interest in presumptive sentencing (Fogel, 1975; Twentieth Century Fund, 1976) and followed, both in style and timing, a major presumptive sentencing proposal put forward by the influential State Bar of Michigan (Committee on Criminal Code Revision, 1977). None of these bills was passed into law because of prosecutorial and judicial resistance to a major change in the substantive criminal code which accompanied presumptive sentencing and a desire to await the outcome of a lengthy sentencing guidelines project conducted under the auspices of the Michigan Supreme Court.

The second kind of general sentencing legislation was mandatory sentencing, and three such bills targeted at specific crimes became law. The first was the felony firearm law. The second was an initiated law to deny good time or special parole to offenders convicted of violent crimes. The third, part of a public health code revision in 1978, was a schedule of draconian penalties for possession of substantial quantities of heroin. Of interest is the fact that each law was conceived by, sponsored by, and became associated with public personages who were openly or quietly seeking nomination as gubernatorial candidates. The drug penalty law, imposing a mandatory life sentence for possession of 650 grams or more of any mixture containing controlled substances such as heroin (and other harsh mandatory sentences) was sponsored by a representative who openly pursued nomination for several years. He also sponsored an expanded electronic eavesdropping law and a reduced bail rights statute before retiring from the State House of Representatives. The initiated law, passed by vote of the people at the 1978 general election, was the result of a massive nomination petition campaign spearheaded by the prosecuting attorney of a large suburban county who is still active in similar campaigns (e.g., a death penalty petition) and openly seeks the governor's office. The felony firearm law was sponsored by the prosecuting attorney of Michigan's most populous county. At a joint legislative committee hearing this prosecutor testified that he had scores of thousands of signatures on petitions supporting the felony firearm bill, which his office in effect had drafted. However, when asked to produce the petition, he refused to do so. The inference was that such a list of signatures and addresses is a potent source of support for anyone seeking statewide elected office.[1]

A rare analysis of legislative politics and the criminal law (Heinz et al., 1969) shows that for the most part criminal legislation is the concern of a small interest group of specialists, public agencies, and occasionally of temporary or ad hoc interest groups. Typically, neither political parties nor elections are important determinants of the outcome of criminal legislation (Heinz et al., 1969: 280). However, we see in Michigan in the late 1970s a situation where sentencing legislation takes on a decidedly political coloration. The rational search for information on crime control became intertwined with the search for votes; the desire to pass effective legislation became enmeshed in the desire to appear tough to the voting public.

LEGISLATION, FACT, AND FANCY

One measure of the rationality of public policy making is the extent to which the policy is responsive to social facts. In an ideal world policy makers would disagree because of differing interests and ideologies but they would at least get their facts straight. In the real world the facts are often garbled, misunderstood, confused, and mixed with rumor and outright lies, especially in situations where executive branch agencies must act promptly (Lippmann, 1922). Legislatures usually move slowly and pass laws only after a series of political maneuvering and fact-finding efforts.

Legislative fact finding is subject to peculiarities that tend to warp objectivity. Public hearings may be structured to draw on testimony prescreened for compatibility with the lawmakers' predilections. Staff members, as generalists, may overlook the most relevant information on an issue. But bias and inefficiency are problems that confront every social policy analyst. When the policy makers are legislators, the problem is exaggerated by the group dynamics of legislators and the disjunction between social facts and legislation.

This problem is described by Edward Levi (1961: 31):

> Despite much gospel to the contrary, a legislature is not a fact-finding body. There is no mechanism, as there is with a court, to require the legislature to sift facts and to make a decision about specific situations. There need be no agreement about what the situation is. The members of the legislative body will be talking about different things; they cannot force each other to accept even a hypothetical set of facts. The result is that even in a non-controversial atmosphere just exactly what has been decided will not be clear.

Levi explicates this proposition through the debate on the Mann Act in 1910, known as the "White Slave Traffic Act." The act was intended to deal with the social problem of innocent young girls being snatched "by bands of 'white slavers' who 'were said to operate from coast to coast, in town and country, with tentacles in foreign lands, east and west and across the American borders.' " The girls were purportedly forced into prostitution and concubinage, would disappear forever from their communities, were brutally whipped and thus became slaves "in the true sense of the word" (Levi, 1961: 34). Undoubted, xenophobia and racism fed interest in the bill as it was said that the most sensational rings were operated by French, Italians, and Jews, and one congressman "told the House the story of a Negro who was supposed to have purchased his third wife 'out of a group of twenty-five that were offered for sale in Chicago' " (Levi, 1961: 37). Yet, for all of this, "there was confusion both as to the facts and as to the legislation proposed" (Levi, 1961: 36). A review of the appellate cases under the Mann Act shows that none dealt with the stereotype envisaged in the debates in Congress. It is entirely conceivable that there never were organized "white slave" rings, or that if there were, whatever abuses of this kind existed were local and sporadic. The point here is that a legislature can pass laws to solve nonexistent social problems, can disregard mathematical laws by declaring that $pi = 3.00$, declare harmless substances to be dangerous and *vice versa,* can establish legislation where the relationship between facts and goals are tenuous, and, generally speaking, enact laws which embody the ruling myths of the day (Arnold, 1962).

LEGISLATIVE CALCULATION

All legislation carries a hypothesis, so to speak, of total effectiveness. It may be supposed, however, that legislators also realize that in practice compliance with a statute is never complete. There are several widely known reasons for the lack of total effectiveness. The inherent inability of a written word formula to be perfectly unambiguous and to foresee every situation to which the law will be applied is an issue that has confronted legal scholars for some time. This is aside from the more mundane problem of sloppy drafting (Dickenson, 1974).

Remington and Rosenblum (1960) expanded our understanding of ambiguous legislation in criminal law by linking ambiguity with discretion. That is, wherever a criminal statute is ambiguous, it creates the possibility, even the need, for discretion by official actors. So, legislatures may purposely write laws that are ambiguous in order to cure specific administrative/enforcement problems, to eliminate potential loopholes, or simply to delegate to administrative agencies the de facto task of defining the criminal activity in question. Such "ambiguity by design" allows legislatures to pass laws without confronting the most controversial issues or without having to think through every conceivable application (Remington and Rosenblum, 1960).

More recently, a law student's comment suggested that a legislative strategy may be undertaken whereby, rather than perceiving noncompliance as diminishing the utility of laws, the noncompliance can be anticipated and thus be used to enhance the utility of laws (Note, 1977). Thus, for example, if a highway traffic speed law is set below the optimal speed, the expected level of noncompliance will produce a socially optimal result. The author posits three necessary preconditions that must be met if a "law that is made to be broken" is a rational strategy for a legislature to pursue. First, the legislature must have at least a rough estimate of the degree of expected noncompliance with the law. Second, the law must be perceived as better achieving its social goals if the predicted level of noncompliance occurs than if there were universal compliance. Third, a benefit-cost analysis must show that the law designed to be broken is a better alternative in terms of efficiency, effectiveness, and justice than full compliance alternatives (Note, 1977: 689-692). After explicating hypothetical laws and offering an ethical defense of this concept, the author shows that the rule of jury nullification is such a law. Namely, it is nearly always put to the jury in absolute terms that they must apply the law as given by the judge. However, for over a century writers have acknowledged that justice may be done on occasion by the practice of jury nullification. Yet jury nullification instructions are resisted because of the rational fear that such instructions would increase the level of nullification above a socially optimal point (Note, 1977: 707-713).

It is instructive that the actual example chosen is one where the law is stated in terms of absolute control over the discretion of a participant in the criminal justice process. Yet the law (a judge-made rule) recognizes, *sub silentio,* a discretion of sorts in the jury to avoid the strictures of the rule in cases where injustice can be avoided. This is not unlike the widespread realization that the substantive criminal law does not eliminate all discretion in the hands of police (Davis, 1969) or prosecutors (Newman, 1966). In other words, while the legislature may desire full compliance with criminal laws aimed at the populace, criminal statutes may be understood, in some sense, as laws that are made to be broken when they guide the action of criminal justice decision makers.

The author acknowledges that an open strategy to enact laws that are made to be broken "has neither been clearly articulated by legal theorists nor methodically pursued by practical lawmakers" (Note, 1977: 687-688). It seems unlikely that a legislature will ever pursue such a policy openly. He justifies laws which appear to deceive the citizenry through the disparity between the law's terms and its goals by relying on a Rawlsian rationale. Persons in the "original position" are rational and aware of the behavioral sciences (Rawls, 1971: 17, 136-138, 143-145, 248-249) and will agree in advance to abide by laws that are made to be broken (Note, 1977: 702-06). This analysis is not practically persuasive. It is far more likely that most citizens will react to such a strategy as they would to Lon Fuller's (1964) lawmaker. A failure of congruence between stated law and its goals is a violation of the rule of law and can be expected to be rejected. But, as the author (Note, 1977) shows by the jury nullification example, a "strategy" of sorts may be pursued by silence.

APPLICATION AND CONCLUSION

Three factors have been presented which partly explain the content and impact of the felony firearm law. In Chapter 4, Bynum notes that the law by its terms strictly controls judicial discretion but leaves prosecutors free to use or disregard it. The political context of the law shows that it was not designed by a cross-section of experts concerned with gun crime control or even by the legislature. It was conceived and popularized by a prosecutor with a possible hidden political agenda. Given the high political visibility of punishment issues, the legislature was apparently in no mood to evaluate the bill critically for its likely impact on gun crime.

In many areas of social and economic policy legislation, including crime and punishment, legislatures have no firmer concept of the link between social facts and outcomes than the society at large. In this country there is a popular view that more severe penalties will deter crime countered by a substantial minority view that rehabilitative programs and improved social conditions will reduce crime. Now there is a growing academic view that the deterrent effect of new programs or penalties over and above those provided for by the existing justice system are likely to have a marginal impact at best. Given this state of confusion, it is little wonder that lawmakers will pass legislation whose backers claim will affect crime rates, especially when such a law appears to carry low implementation costs. The extent of self-delusion in the felony firearm law was far less than in other legislation. If a substantial proportion of the citizenry backs a position over a period of time, that position becomes a ruling myth of society. It is simply asking too much of a legislature supported by a democratic ethos to go against such beliefs.

Finally, it is quite likely that the legislature was aware that the proposed law did not "handcuff" the prosecutors, only the judges. We may hypothesize that the legislature subliminally perceived this as a desirable state of affairs, fearing to impose a law whose mandatory sentencing provisions are so strict that it would cause an explosive crisis in the criminal justice and correctional systems. Thus, rather than being concerned with the opportunity for prosecutorial avoidance, the legislature may have expected, as Bynum clearly showed, that the law would be "mandatory" only when the prosecutor intends it to be mandatory. The concept of laws that are made to be broken (Note, 1977), then, may have a greater applicability than has been realized.

The implementation analysis of a law must go farther back to the text, goals, and politics of the legislation (Berk et al., 1980). This chapter indicates that the rational implementation analyses of the felony firearm law (Bynum, this volume; Loftin and McDowall, 1981), however excellent, will have limited policy impact if they fail to understand the extrarational goals of the legislature and the forces and ways of thinking which constrain legislatures.

It is unlikely that changes will soon be made in the existing felony firearm law, even though the findings of its lack of effectiveness have been made public. Any change is bound to be resisted by the sitting prosecutor who first proposed it, for a change would be a political insult. Prosecutors who regularly ignore the felony firearm law would hesitate to support an amendment that would truly constrain them. The legislature, facing a serious prison overcrowding problem, would be hesitant to pass a law that would exacerbate it.[2] Finally, simple inertia, the press of other business, and the fact that the law's failure has not sunk in make change unlikely. The lesson for impact analysts, if any, is that the policy ramifications of their work is likely to be indirect, affecting other states considering a reform tried elsewhere or generally raising awareness of the need for rational impact analysis prior to passage of laws.

NOTES

1. This account of the testimony and its political ramifications was related to me by a state senator present at the hearing in 1976.
2. It should be noted that some legislation is rational. For example, the Michigan legislature passed a Prison Overcrowding Emergency Powers Act in 1981. The development of the law followed a highly rational process of information gathering, problem solving, and legislative drafting.

REFERENCES

ARNOLD, T. W. (1962) The Symbols of Government. New York: Harcourt Brace Jovanovich.
BERK, R. A., P. BURSTEIN, and I. NAGEL (1980) "Evaluating criminal justice legislation," pp. 611-628 in M. W. Klein and K. S. Teilman (eds.) Handbook of Criminal Justice Evaluation. Beverly Hills, CA: Sage.
Committee on Criminal Code Revision (1977) "Proposed criminal code revision: sentencing the convicted felon." Michigan State Bar J. 56: 121-126.
COOK, P. (1981) "The 'Saturday night special': an assessment of alternative definitions from a policy perspective." J. of Criminal Law and Criminology 72: 1735-1745.
DAVIS, K. C. (1969) Discretionary Justice: A Preliminary Inquiry. Baton Rouge: Louisiana State Univ. Press.
DICKENSON, R. (1974) "Professionalizing legislative drafting: a realistic goal?" Amer. Bar Assoc. J. 60: 562-564.
FEELEY, M. M., A. SARAT, and S. O. WHITE (1977) "The role of state planning in the development of criminal-justice federalism," pp. 204-224 in J. A. Gardiner (ed.) Public Law and Public Policy. New York: Praeger.
FOGEL, D. (1975) . . . We are the living proof . . . Cincinnati: Anderson.
FULLER, L. (1964) The Morality of Law. New Haven: Yale Univ. Press.
HEINZ, J. P., R. W. GETTLEMAN, and M. A. SEESKIN (1969) "Legislative politics and the criminal law." Northwestern Univ. Law Rev. 64: 277-358.

LEVI, E. (1961) An Introduction to Legal Reasoning. Chicago: Phoenix Books.
LIPPMANN, N. W. (1922) Public Opinion. New York: Macmillan.
LOFTIN, C. and D. McDOWALL (1981) " 'One with a gun gets you two': mandatory sentencing and firearm violence in Detroit." Annals of the Amer. Academy of Pol. and Social Sci. 455: 150-167.
NEWMAN, D. J. (1966) Conviction: The Determination of Guilt or Innocence Without Trial. Boston: Little, Brown.
NOTE (1977) "Laws that are made to be broken: adjusting for anticipated noncompliance." Michigan Law Rev. 75: 687-716.
RAWLS, J. (1971) A Theory of Justice. Cambridge, MA: Harvard Univ. Press.
REMINGTON, F. J. and V. G. ROSENBLUM (1960) "The criminal law and the legislative process." Univ. Of Illinois Law Forum 1960: 481-499.
Twentieth Century Fund Task Force on Criminal Sentencing (1976) Fair and Certain Punishment. New York: McGraw-Hill.
ZALMAN, M. (1978) "The rise and fall of the indeterminate sentence." Wayne Law Rev. 24: 857-937.

6

Jack R. Greene

Michigan State University

IMPLEMENTING POLICE PROGRAMS
Some Environmental Impediments

Evaluations of police programs and policies have traditionally focused on police outputs and their ultimate effects. Considerations such as whether crime rates or arrests and clearances are affected by increases in police resource expenditure (Greenwood and Wadycki, 1973; McPheters and Stronge, 1974; Skogan, 1976; Bynum and Cordner, 1980), increases in the actual number of police personnel (Wellford, 1974; Cloninger, 1975; Decker, 1979; and Stahura and Huff, 1979), or through manipulations of certain police practices, most notably patrol (Kelling et al., 1974; Boydstun et al., 1977; Tien et al., 1977; Wilson and Boland, 1978) are illustrative of this evaluation perspective. Allied with this outcome-focused evaluation orientation are studies examining other noncrime effects produced by the police, such as reducing citizen fear of crime, increasing citizen satisfaction with police services, and increasing police-citizen contact and interaction (Boydstun and Sherry, 1975).

Generally, the results of effects-oriented evaluations of police programs and policies have been disappointing, failing to link systematically the inputs of policing (resources, more officers, public support) to police

AUTHOR'S NOTE: *This chapter is a revised version of a paper presented at the 1981 conference of the American Society of Criminology, Washington, D.C. This research was partially supported under Grant No. 77-NI-99-0028, Office of Criminal Justice Education and Training, Law Enforcement Assistance Administration, U.S. Department of Justice. I wish to thank Gary W. Cordner of the University of Baltimore for his review and comments on earlier drafts. Victoria Schneider of Michigan State University provided library research assistance.*

71

outcomes. Such inability to demonstrate the causal links between inputs and outputs is disconcerting for a number of reasons. First, the results of such study generally support the null hypothesis or the conclusion of no difference. If such a conclusion is warranted, it must first be demonstrated that, indeed, the programs were put into practice as intended. Without such a demonstration it is unknown whether the program failed due to overadvocacy (Campbell, 1972), an inability to achieve proximate goals (Suchman, 1969), or because of instrumental failure or poor theory (Kerr, 1976). Second, and of equal concern, is the problem of attributing the causes of "success" to programs that have achieved their desired ends. Without a firm understanding of the implementation of such policies or programs, the ability to generalize police programs from one city to another is severely circumscribed.

In a review of the police crime effectiveness literature, Wycoff (1982) suggests that the absence of conclusive information on the ability of the police to achieve crime-related objectives is related to poor conceptualization of crime effectiveness, poor measurement of the behaviors of the police which might account for the presence or absence of effectiveness, and an overreliance on aggregate analysis which masks the conversion processes linking police inputs to outcomes. Such a criticism strikes at the differences between *policy analysis* and *implementation analysis*. The former implies assessment of the ultimate ends and likely consequences, and the latter examines the "institutional means of achieving such effects" (Hargrove, 1975).

In recent years evaluation research in a number of public agency settings has begun to explore the conversion of policy to practice (Murphy, 1971; Derthick, 1972, 1976; Pressman and Wildavsky, 1973; Williams, 1976). In law enforcement, the process of implementing policy and the effect of organizational factors on policy implementation have gained recent attention (Lewis and Greene, 1978). As evaluation studies in policing have found little or no difference in outcomes, researchers have shifted their attention inward to the police organization.

For example, Wycoff and Kelling (1978) found that a general lack of goal consensus, rising internal expectations, and resistance from police supervisors combined effectively to thwart efforts to introduce change in personnel policy in a major city police department. Similarly, other researchers have identified police officers as impediments to altering the rank structure of American police agencies (Guyot, 1979); have found middle- and upper-management resistance to community-based policing projects (Schwartz and Clarren, 1977); and have found such factors as lack of goal consensus, perceptions of threat and influence, and feelings of dependence to affect the acceptance and use of police projects (Greene, 1981a). Cumulatively, these studies point to the dynamic nature of the internal and external environments of police agencies (Sandler and Mintz, 1974) and to the forces affecting police policy implementation.

Understanding the effect of police agency and environmental factors on the implementation of law enforcement programs requires an open systems frame of reference. All organizations, including police agencies, can be characterized as open systems, importing some form of energy (e.g., raw materials, people, or information) from the environment, converting this energy through some form of technology, and then returning this converted output to the environment for consumption (Perrow, 1970). In law enforcement, environmental energy might consist of normative support through public opinion, information on crime and criminal suspects, or fiscal support through public budgets. Conversion can take place through patrol strategies, the use of follow-up investigations, or police-community relations. The resulting output, presumably, would include the quality of the police service provided.

Interactions with the environment is not passive, however. Often this interaction affects how the organization defines its goals (Thompson and McEwen, 1958), and the degree of autonomy of organizational leaders (Dill, 1958). Public outcry over a particularly heinous crime, for example, can turn a passive environment into an aggressive one, dramatically affecting police policy decisions (Greene, 1981b). In policing, the environment also includes such elements as the prosecutor, the courts, public opinion and ideology, legal, social, and cultural norms, fiscal and economic conditions, and competition between agencies for scarce public resources, to name but a few. Each of these factors has the potential for creating support or opposition for police policies and for their implementation.

Police organizations can also be characterized as having an internal environment consisting of such attributes as a division of labor and functional specialization, locus of authority and decision making, formalized roles and practices, and individual organizational members socialized to certain organizational routines. These internal attributes are themselves in a dynamic state, with individuals and organizational units often competing with one another for organizational prestige and reward and responding differentially to various aspects of the external environment (Thompson, 1967; Lawrence and Lorsch, 1969). Internal environmental considerations in law enforcement also include the relationships between the various functional divisions of the agency (patrol versus investigations), the degree of vested interest individuals within the organization have in maintaining existing practice (Lewis and Greene, 1978), differences in the various organizational technologies for dealing with the environment (preventive patrol versus follow-up investigations), and agreement about the goals, objectives, and operational strategies of the organization.

Obviously, many factors can contribute to the failure to implement a particular police policy. External pressures prohibiting certain types of police decoy practices may result in failure to sustain such efforts. Internal dissensus over the methods of policing (random patrol versus split force), or the ultimate goals of police efforts (crime prevention versus crime suppression), may result in policy implementation failure as well. Further, assumptions about how the conversion is to take place (through police specialists or police generalists) may contribute to policy failure in law enforcement. As prior research has concentrated on police outputs and the ultimate effects of such policy interventions, little is known about the degree to which these sundry factors influence policy implementation.

Law enforcement administrators and evaluators must be cognizant of agency environments (internal and external) and the consequences of each for the implementation process. Factors external to the police agency, such as public opinion or ideology, are indeed difficult to predict with great certainty. Despite the uncertainty these factors represent, implementation evaluations can take into account certain aspects of the external environment, such as the set of organizations most likely to interact with the police agency (Evan, 1966) and the relationships among organizations in the wider environment (Warren, 1967; Turk, 1970).

Internal organizational environments, while also posing a certain degree of uncertainty, have been demonstrated to affect the implementation of social programs in general, as well as in law enforcement in particular. For example, in assessing the implementation of educational policies, Berman and Pauly (1975: ix) indicate:

> The effective implementation of innovative projects depended primarily upon a supportive institutional setting and on an implementation strategy that fostered the mutual adaptation of the staff to the project's demands and of the project's design to the reality of its setting.

Such concerns for implementing educational policy are echoed by Wycoff and Kelling (1978: 73) in assessing the implementation failure of a policy aimed at reforming police personnel practices:

> The consequence of the need to begin [the programs] was a lack of time for management to assess organizational response to the pro-

grams and to plan implementation strategies. The pressures of program management and the heat of conflict did not allow for the reasoned development of strategies which could extend beyond fighting bush fires and clubbing alligators.

Implementation assessment, then, begins with an analysis of the institutional means for achieving desired ends, and it requires an organizational frame of reference. The current study examines the implementation of three types of police policies: (1) visible saturation patrol, attempting to enhance the police agency's general deterrent effect; (2) undercover surveillance, focused on individual deterrence through apprehension; and (3) regionalized detective bureaus, designed to increase the follow-up investigation capability of the police agencies involved. While the police projects examined differed in their focus (e.g., saturation patrol, undercover surveillance, follow-up investigation), each required implementation into a hosting police agency or group of police agencies. Consequently, each project can be viewed as a separate organization interacting with a wider environment. In certain instances this environment was within a single police agency where the specialized project interacted with other organizational subunits, such as patrol and detective units. In other instances, projects implemented in multiple agencies encountered more complex environments composed of numerous patrol and detective units. The police interventions analyzed here are assessed not for their ultimate effect, as the broader evaluation effort found no differences in the effects achieved (Lewis et al., 1977). Rather, the concern in this study is to identify the antecedents to police policy effectiveness—namely, environmental processes affecting the implementation of such policies.

METHOD

Sampling

The current study was part of a broader evaluation effort designed to examine 25 specialized police projects funded by LEAA which attempted to introduce significant policy changes in the participating police organizations. These projects, as previously indicated, can be aggregated over three separate intervention strategies, (1) saturation patrol, (2) undercover surveillance, and (3) regionalized follow-up investigations. Six of these specialized police projects, two from each of the above categories, were selected for intensive evaluation; the results reported here are from the six intensive evaluation sites.

Data were collected through the use of a survey instrument distributed to people who held the following role/positions within these organizations: (1) commander of patrol unit, (2) patrol officer, (3) commander of investigation or detective unit, and (4) detective. In all, a total of 817 surveys were distributed throughout the 21 police agencies participating in these projects; 450 were returned for a response rate of 55 percent. Of those returned, 379 form the basis of analysis for this inquiry.[1]

Measurement

Survey items were constructed using a modified Likert-type response set. This chapter examines the effects of seven environmental variables on three measures of implementation outcome. The environmental variables are broken down into three groups.

The first group of variables measured environmental perceptions of goal consensus, dependence, and threat posed by the introduction of special police units into existing organizational and environmental relationships. Goal consensus was measured by asking respondents to indicate the extent to which commanders and administrators within their police agency actively supported the goals of the special police projects. Dependence was measured by asking respondents to express the extent to which their jobs and their knowledge of crime and criminal activity in their jurisdiction were affected by the special police unit project. Threat perception was inferred from a survey item asking about respondent trust of individuals in the special unit.

The second group of variables examined management of the environment. They include perceptions of cooperation fostered by personnel in the special units toward those in the environment (cooperation), perceptions about the degree to which the respondent's agency or organizational subunit had influence in the policy making of the special unit (cooptation), and respondent identification of formal policies requiring that others in patrol and investigations interact with the special unit (coordination).

The third category of variables measured the nature of the environment confronted by the police projects studied. This measurement was guided by a framework developed by Warren (1967), who specified differences between environmental contexts based on such dimensions as locus of authority and decision making, relations of units, structural provisions of the division of labor, commitment to leadership subsystems, and the orientation of the collectivity. Using this approach respondents in the six specialized police projects were classified as being in a unitary, federative, or coalitional environmental context.

The unitary context is typically found within a single organization, where the goals, authority structure, and hierarchy are inclusive. Two of the police projects were conducted within single organizations and were classified as confronting a unitary environment. Two other police projects were classified as being involved in a federative environment, where there were often disparate organizational goals but formal organization for the special unit's goals, where the decision-making structure was subject to ratification of the participating agencies, and where police agencies brought personnel together for the purpose of the particular police intervention. These two projects required the participation of seven police agencies (four in one and three in the other) to form covert surveillance units. Each participating unit retained some control over the police personnel it assigned to the special unit, yet the unit maintained its own authority structure and division of labor. The final two police projects involved the participation of a large number of police agencies, often in one or more counties, to form regionalized investigation units. These two projects were classified as being within a coalitional environment, in part due to the numbers of agencies involved and in part because each participating agency retained a greater degree of autonomy in the relationship than was the case for agencies in the federative context.

Three measures of implementation are included in the analysis. Integration into environmental networks was measured through assessments of the extent to which the special unit was viewed as having continuing cooperative relationships with other organizational subunits or other police agencies (integration). The ultimate effectiveness of these special units was measured by respondent agreement that the special police unit had affected how the organization(s) handled crime (impact). Finally, use was measured by respondent reports of the frequency of interaction with the special police projects, either by providing information to the unit or by requesting and receiving information from the unit (use).

Analysis

Each of the implementation outcome variables (integration, impact, and use) is used as the dependent variable in multiple regression analyses of the extent to which environmental factors affect special police unit implementation. For each implementation outcome variable, there were two steps in the analysis. The first considers the relationship between all of the independent variables and the implementation outcome. To do this, two dummy variables—one measuring the unitary environmental context and the other representing the coalitional context—were constructed and are included in the regression equation. The second step is individual regression analyses for each environmental context, attempting to control statistically for environmental context as a factor affecting police policy implementation.

Table 6.1 presents the zero-order correlations between the variables used in subsequent regression analyses. Moderate to strong correlations were found between certain of the environmental variables and the implementation outcomes. For example, as presented in Table 6.1, higher respondent perceptions of dependence on the activities of the special unit were associated with more positive evaluations of impact (.64), integration (.43), and use (.32). These same respondents (high dependence) perceived less threat (-.46) in the establishment of the special unit and were higher in their assessments of cooperation (.57). Similarly, assessments of use of the special unit were found to be positively correlated with beliefs about integration (.46) and impact (.35) and negatively correlated with perceptions of threat (-.27). Environmental contexts were not found to be correlated with implementation outcome variables. Formal coordination was found to be positively associated with the coalitional environmental context (.26) while negatively associated with the unitary environment (-.29). Neither of these associations is particularly strong, however.

While the interrelationships between individual environmental variables and the implementation outcomes are instructive, the concern here is with the effects of each of these factors as they impede or facilitate policy implementation. Pursuing this question, Table 6.2 presents the results of regression analyses of the environmental variables (independent variables) on each of the three implementation outcomes (dependent variables). As shown in column 1 of Table 6.2, three variables were found to be highly and significantly predictive of special unit integration. Respondent's high assessments of special unit integration were associated with perceptions of cooperative relationships with the special unit, job dependence on special unit efforts, and goal consensus. With regard to assessments of special unit impact (column 2 of Table 6.2), the results are similar to those reported for integration, with higher perceptions of dependence and cooperation associated with higher evaluations of impact. Interestingly, in analyzing impact, it is found that the higher the perception of cooptation, the higher the assessment of impact. This finding indicates that perceptions of both

TABLE 6.1 Zero-Order Correlation Coefficients for Environmental and Implementation Outcome Variables

	(1)	(2)	(3)	(4)	(5)	(6)	(7)	(8)	(9)	(10)	(11)
Integration	.46										
Impact	.35	.54									
Goal Concensus	.20	.34	.32								
Dependence	.32	.43	.64	.23							
Threat Perception	-.27	-.50	-.57	-.35	-.46						
Cooperation	.32	.60	.71	.36	.57	-.74					
Cooptation	.28	.38	.43	.23	.29	-.45	.51				
Coordination	.30	.29	.31	.27	.23	-.23	.36	.18			
Unitary Context	-.03	.04	.00	.05	.04	-.06	.04	.07	-.29		
Federative Context	-.04	-.04	-.08	-.10	-.03	-.03	-.05	-.11	.00	-.38	
Coalitional Context	.06	.01	.06	.05	.01	.07	.08	.04	.26	-.56	-.55

(1) Use
(2) Integration
(3) Impact
(4) Goal Consensus
(5) Dependence
(6) Threat Perception
(7) Cooperation
(8) Cooptation
(9) Coordination
(10) Unitary Context
(11) Federative Context

TABLE 6.2   Multiple Regression Analysis of Environmental Factors
Affecting Implementation Outcomes

	Standardized Regression Coefficients		
Environmental Factor	With Integration Dependent	With Impact Dependent	With Use Dependent
Goal consensus	.12[a]	.05	.05
Dependence	.12[a]	.35[a]	.19[a]
Threat perception	-.09	-.05	-.04
Cooperation	.36[a]	.39[a]	.01
Cooptation	.08	.08[a]	.15[a]
Coordination	.08	.04	.20[a]
Unitary context (dummy variable)	.03	.01	.01
Coalitional context (dummy variable)	-.01	.03	-.00
R^2	.41	.59	.19
F	31.84[a]	66.71[a]	10.64[a]

[a] $p < .01$

cooperation and influence in policy making (cooptation) are important for assessments of impact.

In contrast to the findings regarding assessments of integration and impact, the findings for use (column 3, Table 6.2) suggest that coordination, cooptation, and perceptions of dependence are more predictive of use than are other environmental variables, most notably cooperation. In this regard, the analyses in Table 6.2 suggest that cooperation is less important in determining the use of special police units by those in the environment than it is for assessments of integration and impact. It is also interesting to note in Table 6.2 that while each of the regression equations is successful in accounting for a relatively large amount of the variance in the dependent variables, the equation predicting use is less successful (R^2 = .19 versus .41 and .59), than are those predicting integration and impact. The dummy variable measures of external environmental context were not found to be significant in any of the regression analyses.

Extending our consideration of the effects of various environmental variables on implementation outcomes, Tables 6.3 through 6.5 were constructed. Each table represents separate regression analyses of each of the

TABLE 6.3   Multiple Regression Analysis of Environmental Factors Affecting Special Police *Integration*

	Standardized Regression Coefficients		
Environmental Factor	For Unitary Context	For Federative Context	For Coalitional Context
Goal consensus	.08	.20[a]	.10
Dependence	-.06	.15	.25[b]
Threat perception	-.09	-.12	-.04
Cooperation	.47[b]	.33[b]	.30[b]
Cooptation	.07	-.02	.16[a]
Coordination	.09	.07	.03
R^2	.38	.42	.45
F	10.15[b]	11.42[b]	22.20[b]
	N = 106	N = 103	N = 169

[a] $p < .05$
[b] $p < .01$

dependent variables (integration, impact, and use), for each type of external environmental context (unitary, federative, and coalitional).

As shown in Table 6.3, differing organizational factors and management strategies were found to be significant for predicting special police unit integration depending on the environmental context confronting the unit. For example, throughout all contexts, the higher the assessment of cooperation, the higher the assessment of integration. However, goal consensus was significant for integration in the federative environmental context but not in either the unitary or coalitional. Similarly, perceptions of dependence and cooptation were significant in predicting assessments of integration in the coalitional context but not in the unitary or federative. Such findings tend to support the idea that the nature of the external environment affects implementation outcomes.

Table 6.4 examines the effects of the independent variables on assessments of special unit impact for each type of external environmental context. As shown in Table 6.4, the results of the analysis are consistent across environmental contexts. In each context, the higher the perceptions of dependence and cooperation, the higher the assessments of impact. One exception to this trend is noted in Table 6.4. In the coalitional environmental context, it was found that the higher the perceptions of coopta-

TABLE 6.4   Multiple Regression Analysis of Environmental Factors
Affecting Assessments of Special Police Unit *Impact*

	Standardized Regression Coefficients		
Environmental Factor	For Unitary Context	For Federative Context	For Coalitional Context
Goal consensus	-.02	.10	.04
Dependence	.30[b]	.25[b]	.43[b]
Threat perception	-.13	-.01	-.06
Cooperation	.46[b]	.49[b]	.30[b]
Cooptation	-.02	.04	.14[b]
Coordination	-.11	.05	.09
R^2	.52	.56	.67
F	17.81[b]	20.76[b]	55.99[a]
	N = 106	N = 103	N = 169

[a] $p < .05$
[b] $p < .01$

tion, the higher the assessments of impact. This variable was not significant
in either the unitary or federative environmental contexts.

In the analysis of Table 6.2 it was indicated that the variables predictive
of assessments of integration and impact were not necessarily the same in
the prediction of use. The analysis reported in Table 6.5 supports this
conclusion. As is shown in Table 6.5, differing variables within the three
external environmental contexts are significant for self-reported use. For
example, in the unitary context, the variable measuring coordination is the
only significant variable in the equation, indicating that the higher the
assessment of coordination, the higher the use. By contrast, in the federative context, cooptation is significant and positive. Finally, in the coalitional context, dependence and coordination are positive and significant in
accounting for use. Thus, the various environmental variables identified
(goal consensus, dependence, threat perception) and the particular type of
implementation management strategies (cooperation, cooptation, coordination) were found to account for implementation differentially (integration, impact, use) depending on the type of external environmental
context.

TABLE 6.5   Multiple Regression Analysis of Environmental Factors Affecting Special Police Unit *Use*

	Standardized Regression Coefficients		
Environmental Factor	For Unitary Context	For Federative Context	For Coalitional Context
Goal consensus	.10	.07	.01
Dependence	.09	.15	.29[b]
Threat perception	.06	-.04	-.10
Cooperation	.16	-.00	-.11
Cooptation	.11	.26[a]	.13
Coordination	.23[a]	.15	.23[b]
R^2	.17	.20	.21
F	3.42[b]	4.01[b]	7.29[b]
	N = 106	N = 103	N = 169

[a] $p < .05$
[b] $p < .01$

DISCUSSION

Analyses of the effects of selected environmental variables on aspects of the implementation of police policy have important implications. First, tne results are consistent with previous understandings of complex organizations and the forces that affect organizations. In this regard, the analyses presented suggest that strategies used by organizations to gain some acceptance and, hence, control over an uncertain environment are themselves affected by the type of environment confronted (Thompson, 1967). In the police agencies studied, the strategy of environmental cooperation was found to be important in each of the contexts examined when the primary issues were assessments of integration and impact of the special police units. When use of the special unit was at issue, the method of environmental management shifted from informal cooperation toward more formalized methods of interaction among organizations. In this regard, formal coordination was found to be the most significant factor in explaining use of special units in both the unitary and coalitional environmental contexts, while cooptation was found to be the most significant in the federative context.

These findings are consistent with organizational theory and with what we know about police agencies. For example, formal coordination is perhaps the method most often used to coordinate work in a single organization where the organizational subunits all fall under the same authority and decision-making structure (Thompson, 1967; Blau, 1974). And in police work within a single agency, formal coordination of work units is often required, as informal coordination of police activities rarely occurs with much success. Such intraorganizational problems in law enforcement as secret information (Bittner, 1970; Manning, 1978; Rubenstein, 1973), status differences between investigators and patrol officers (Niederhoffer, 1967: 83-84), and the maintenance of social and personal distance between investigators and patrol officers (Sanders, 1977) contribute to a breakdown in informal intraorganizational coordinative efforts. This being the case, the formal requirements for coordination may ultimately reduce the likelihood that organizational members may verbally support the implementation of a new organizational unit but not feel compelled to interact with it.

In the coalitional context, where perceptions of dependence were also found to account for special police unit use, the vastness of the number of possible interactions with such large numbers of police personnel involved may require formal coordination, if for no other reason than to routinize the interaction patterns. Also, regarding the coalitional environment, it should be remembered that such a context affords a great deal of autonomy among participating units (Warren, 1967). Such autonomy, similar to the autonomy between patrol and investigations in the single organization, may require formal statements about interaction for precisely the same reasons. Such statements, coupled with actual perceptions of dependence, may help cement the coalition. These results for special police units are consistent with those found by Selznick's (1966) analysis of the Tennessee Valley Authority, a semipublic coalition of government and local interests which viewed the coalition as highly interdependent and which developed numerous formal coordinative methods.

The finding that cooptation was most significant in explaining use of the special police units in the federative environmental context is also consistent with what is known about organizations and police work. With respect to organizations, federations require a greater participation in the structuring of the relationships between the subunits (Warren, 1967), because by participating in the federation these organizations give up a great deal of autonomy and control over the unit. Expectations of participation are therefore consistent with a social exchange perspective (Blau, 1974) in which the organization expects influence in decision making as a condition to giving up autonomy. As police work has itself been characterized as an exchange process (Manning, 1978), the expectation that those who perceived input and influence into the specialized police project would also see themselves as committed to carrying out the project by using the special unit is consistent with our previous discussions.

The second set of implications from this study relate to the environmental variables studied. From this analysis the following observations are relevant: Perceptions of dependence greatly affect assessments of integration and impact and to a lesser extent use; goal consensus influences implementation; and perceptions of threat had very little influence on implementation outcomes.

Such findings are consistent with previous research on organizations and policing. With respect to organizations, goal consensus has been suggested as an important consideration in the provision of medical care and social services (Levine et al., 1963) and in education (Clark, 1965). Goal consensus has also been suggested as important for implementing structural changes within police agencies (Greene, 1981a). The nature of the individual, entrepreneurial role of the police officer also suggests that negotiation and exchange are the basic methods of interaction within the police milieu (Bittner, 1970), and that such orientations can be expected to carry over to individual officer assessments of new policies and how they will be implemented in police agencies. Thus, individual officer assessments of the implementation of special police units might well be expected to be influenced by such concerns as dependence, threat perception, or efforts to negotiate environmental relationships (cooperation, cooptation, and coordination). Such organizational assessments are consistent with the analysis of change in the Dallas Police Department (Wycoff and Kelling, 1978), where middle managers were threatened by the innovation and consequently subverted change, and within the community-based policing effort of the Cincinnati Police Department (Schwartz and Clarren, 1977), where central administrators effectively thwarted successful implementation. These analyses are also consistent with evaluations of numerous team policing projects, particularly with respect to why they failed (Sherman et al., 1973).

Cumulatively, these findings suggest the importance of environmental variables as they affect the implementation process directly—and, of course, as they potentially affect the ultimate outcome of police policy interventions. Without such analysis these antecedent links between policy statements and practice are unknown. The study of implementation in the policy-making process is critical, for as Pressman and Wildavsky tell us:

> When we say that programs have failed, this suggests that we are surprised. If we thought from the beginning that they were unlikely to be successful, their failure to achieve stated goals or to work at all would not cry out for any special explanation. If we believed that intense conflicts of interest were involved, if people who had to cooperate were expected to be at loggerheads, if necessary resources were far beyond those available, we might wonder rather more why the programs were attempted instead of expressing amazement at their shortcomings [1973: 87].

NOTE

1. Seventy-one of the returned responses were incomplete in one or more of the variables of interest. The regression analyses employed a listwise deletion procedure where cases were omitted from consideration if information on any of the pertinent variables was found missing (see Nie et al., 1975: 353).

REFERENCES

BERMAN, P. and E. PAULY (1975) Federal Programs Supporting Educational Change, Volume II: Factors Affecting Change Agency Projects. Santa Monica, CA: Rand.

BITTNER, E. (1970) The Functions of the Police in Modern Society. Rockville, MD: National Institute of Mental Health.

BLAU, P. (1974) On the Nature of Organizations. New York: John Wiley.

BOYDSTUN, J. E. and M. E. SHERRY (1975) San Diego Community Profile—Final Report. Washington, DC: Police Foundation.

——— and N. P. MOELTEN (1977) Patrol Staffing in San Diego. Washington, DC: Police Foundation.

BYNUM, T. S. and G. W. CORDNER (1980) "Crime rates and police employment." Presented at the meeting of the Midwestern Association of Criminal Justice Educators, Chicago.

CAMPBELL, D. T. (1972) "Reforms as experiments," pp. 187-223 in C. Weiss (ed.) Evaluating Action Programs: Readings in Social Action and Education. Boston: Allyn & Bacon.

CLARK, B. R. (1965) "Interorganizational patterns in education." Admin. Sci. Q. 10: 224-237.

CLONINGER, D. O. (1975) "The deterrent effect of law enforcement: an evaluation of recent findings and some new evidence." Amer. J. of Economics and Sociology 34: 323-335.

DECKER, S. H. (1979) "Allocating police resources and fluctuating crime rates," pp. 97-112 in D. M. Peterson (ed.) Police Work. Beverly Hills, CA: Sage.

DERTHICK, M. (1976) "Washington: angry citizens and an ambitious plan," pp. 219-242 in W. Williams and R. F. Elmore (eds.) Social Program Implementation. New York: Academic Press.

——— (1972) New Towns In-Town: Why a Federal Program Failed. Washington, DC: Urban Institute.

DILL, W. R. (1958) "Environment as an influence on managerial autonomy." Admin. Sci. Q. 2: 409-443.

EVAN, W. M. (1966) "The organizational set: toward a theory of interorganizational relations," pp. 201-228 in J. D. Thompson (ed.) Approaches to Organizational Design. Pittsburg: Univ. of Pittsburg Press.

GREENE, J. R. (1981a) "Organizational change in law enforcement." J. of Criminal Justice 9: 79-91.

——— (1981b) "The environment of manpower decision making," pp. 180-208 in J. K. Hudzik, T. S. Bynum, G. W. Cordner, K. M. Christian, and S. M. Edwards, Criminal Justice Manpower Planning: An Overview. Washington, DC: Government Printing Office.

GREENWOOD, M. J. and W. J. WADYCKI (1973) "Crime rates and public expenditures for police protection: their interaction." Rev. of Social Economy 31: 138-151.

GUYOT, D. (1979) "Bending granite: attempts to change the rank structure of American police departments." J. of Police Sci. and Admin. 7: 243-284.

HARGROVE, E. C. (1975) The Missing Link: The Study of Implementation in Social Policy. Washington, DC: Urban Institute.

KERR, D. H. (1976) "The logic of 'policy' and successful policies." Policy Sciences 7: 351-363.

KELLING, G. L., T. PATE, D. DIECKMAN, and C. E. BROWN (1974) The Kansas City Preventive Patrol Experiment—A Summary Report. Washington, DC: Police Foundation.

LAWRENCE, P. R. and J. W. LORSCH (1969) Developing Organizations: Diagnosis and Action. Reading, MA: Addison-Wesley.

LEVINE, S., P. E. WHITE, and B. D. PAUL (1963) "Community interorganizational problems in providing medical care and social services." Amer. J. of Public Health 53: 1183-1195.

LEWIS, R. G. and J. R. GREENE (1978) "Implementation evaluation: a future direction in project evaluation." J. of Criminal Justice 6: 167-176.

——— and S. EDWARDS (1977) Specialized Police Units in Michigan: An Evaluation. Lansing, MI: Office of Criminal Justice Programs.

McPHETERS, L. R. and W. B. STRONGE (1974) "Law enforcement expenditures and urban crime." National Tax J. 27: 633-644.

MANNING, P. K. (1978) "Lying, secrecy and social control," pp. 238-254 in P. K. Manning and J. Van Maanen (eds.) Policing: A View from the Street. Santa Monica, CA: Goodyear.

MURPHY, J. T. (1971) "Title I of ESEA: the politics of implementing federal education reform." Harvard Business Rev. 41: 35-63.

NIE, N. H., C. H. HULL, J. G. JENKINS, K. STEINBRENNER, and D. H. BENT (1975) Statistical Package for the Social Sciences. New York: McGraw-Hill.

NIEDERHOFFER, A. (1967) Behind the Shield: The Police in Urban Society. New York: Anchor.

PERROW, C. (1970) Organizational Analysis: A Sociological View. Monterey, CA: Brooks/Cole.

PRESSMAN, J. L. and A. B. WILDAVSKY (1973) Implementation. Berkeley: Univ. of California Press.

RUBENSTEIN, J. (1973) City Police. New York: Ballantine.

SANDERS, W. (1977) Detective Work. New York: Free Press.

SANDLER, G. and E. MINTZ (1974) "Police organizations: their changing internal and external relationships." J. of Police Sci. and Admin. 4: 458-463.

SCHWARTZ, A. I. and S. N. CLARREN (1977) The Cincinnati Team Policing Experiment: A Summary Report. Washington, DC: Urban Institute/Police Foundation.

SELZNICK, P. (1966) TVA and The Grass Roots: A Study in the Sociology of Formal Organizations. New York: Harper & Row.

SHERMAN, L. W., C. H. MILTON, and T. V. KELLY (1973) Team Policing: Seven Case Studies. Washington, DC: Police Foundation.

SKOGAN, W. G. (1976) "Efficiency and effectiveness in big city police departments." Public Admin. Rev. 36: 278-286.

STAHURA, J. M. and R. C. HUFF (1979) "Crime and police employment," pp. 79-96 in D. Peterson (ed.) Police Work. Beverly Hills, CA: Sage.

SUCHMAN, E. A. (1969) "Evaluating educational programs: a symposium." Urban Rev. 4.

THOMPSON, J. D. (1967) Organizations in Action. New York: McGraw-Hill.

——— and W. J. McEWEN (1958) "Organizational goals and environment: goal setting as an interaction process." Amer. Soc. Rev. 23: 23-31.

TIEN, J., J. SIMON, and R. LARSON (1977) An Alternative Approach in Police Patrol: The Wilmington Split-Force Experiment. Cambridge, MA: Public Systems Evaluations.

TURK, H. (1970) "Interorganizational networks in urban society: initial perspectives and comparative research." Amer. Soc. Rev. 35: 1-19.

WARREN, R. L. (1967) "The interorganizational field as a focus for investigation." Admin. Sci. Q. 23: 396-419.

WELLFORD, C. R. (1974) "Crime and the police: a multivariate analysis." Criminology 12: 195-213.

WILLIAMS, W. (1976) Social Policy Research and Analysis. New York: American Elsevier.

WILSON, J. Q. and B. BOLAND (1978) "The effect of the police on crime." Law and Society Rev. 12: 367-390.

WYCOFF, M. A. (1982) "Evaluating the crime effectiveness of municipal police," pp. 15-36 in J. R. Greene (ed.) Managing Police Work: Issues and Analysis. Beverly Hills, CA: Sage.

——— and G. L. KELLING (1978) The Dallas Experience—Organizational Reform. Washington, DC: Police Foundation.

7

Craig H. Blakely
William S. Davidson II
Michigan State University

PROBLEMS IN IMPLEMENTATION
The Demonstration Project Model

A **phenomenon** of considerable conceptual concern is the viability of the research, development, and dissemination (RD&D) model as a usable vehicle in the development of innovative criminal justice programs. The utility of this model is of paramount concern in the process of policy formation and implementation. This chapter will attempt to dissect this phenomenon further by viewing the issue from the perspective of an adopting juvenile court's impact on the intervention process of an innovative juvenile diversion program.

The classic RD&D model (Havelock, 1969) served as both a research paradigm and a social policy model. The model calls for the development of an innovative technology in response to an existing social problem. The effectiveness of this new technology is then determined through formative and summative evaluation of a demonstration project. Typically, the innovative new program is experimentally compared with a no-treatment or state-of-the-art control group. If the demonstration project (and frequently some systematic replication) proves to have impact on alleviating the given social problem, the new technology then becomes accepted practice. Criminal justice service agencies are viewed as adopters in the

AUTHORS' NOTE: This work was completed under Grant No MH29160 from the Center for the Studies of Crime and Delinquency, National Institute of Mental Health.

RD&D process who value evaluation results and passively receive program-matic innovations. Thus, the classic RD&D model ultimately calls for the dissemination of the innovation and/or information about the innovation to individuals and organizations that have contact with the social problem.

However, there is increased concern about the effectiveness and efficiency of this model (Williams, 1976). Evidence has accumulated suggesting that adopting organizations are not passive recipients of disseminated programs (House, 1981; Berman and McLaughlin, 1978). Rather, a multitude of factors influence the degree to which adopting organizations incorporate innovations with high fidelity. Frequently adopters appear to reinvent the model innovation to fit their own problematic or political needs (Eveland et al., 1977). Since the degree to which the adopting organization implements an innovation can vary, the critical components of the original innovation might also be lost, reducing effectiveness.

It is within the context of these issues that we will address the notion of policy impact. By examining implementation, the current research addresses a major problem facing the research and development model currently in vogue. More specifically, the research examines the generalization of the activities of a model diversion program (Davidson, 1976; Davidson et al., 1977) following the transference of operational supervision to an existing community agency.

HISTORICAL PERSPECTIVE

In the early 1970s, the Adolescent Diversion Project was developed to provide an alternative to the juvenile justice system for adolescents who had come into formal contact with the system (Rappaport et al., 1979). Youths who would normally have been petitioned to the juvenile court were referred directly to the program by local police departments. Under-graduate social science majors were utilized as direct service providers. Students received eight to ten weeks of intense training in the techniques of behavioral contracting (Stuart, 1971) and child advocacy (Davidson and Rapp, 1976). Students spent the remainder of their nine-month commitment in direct provision of services to referred youths. The general model called for an initial assessment period of several weeks. During this period, the volunteers spent their time getting to know the youths, meeting significant others in the youths' life, and setting general intervention goals. During the first several weeks a good deal of time was spent in recreational activities allowing for interpersonal interaction necessary in the assessment phase. Following assessment, more detailed intervention goals were specified and actual intervention activities increased. During the last several weeks of the intervention period, the volunteers reduced their direct involvement in intervention activities and increasingly returned control of the situation to the youths and their families. Throughout the intervention interval, the youth and his or her family were encouraged to advocate on their own behalf and negotiate their own behavioral contracts with decreasing input from the student volunteer. During this period, concomitant with the reduced level of direct intervention related activities, the student volunteers were expected to increase the proportion of time invested in recreational activities.

The project was evaluated extensively in an effort to discern the essential components that had produced positive outcomes. Typically, demonstration project evaluations of innovative technologies merely asked the question, "Does it work?" The more complex question of what components of the model are responsible for the desired outcome are seldom addressed (Emshoff et al., 1980). This unfortunate state of affairs, coupled with the observation that adopting organizations frequently do not adopt the innovation per se, but in fact adapt the technology (Charters and Jones, 1973), leads one to conclude that "tinkering with the innovation may effect the critical components responsible for its success" (Emshoff et al., 1980: 2).

The current research attempted to explore this dissemination process. More specifically, within the confines of a true experimental design, the extent to which an adopting organization reinvented the innovation during implementation was assessed.

METHOD

This study took place within the context of a five-year research project funded by the National Institute of Mental Health. A local county juvenile court serving a medium-sized Midwestern city served as the referral source for delinquent youths.

Youth Referred

The 23 youths involved in the research averaged 14.5 years of age. Two-thirds of the youths were white and two-thirds were male. All socioeconomic strata were represented; however, lower- and middle-income groups were predominant. Petitions on referred youths included those for minor and serious misdemeanors as well as minor felonies. Status offenders were not referred to the program. The youths were randomly assigned to treatment conditions.

Nonprofessional Volunteers

Eleven male and 12 female undergraduates at a large Midwestern university served as project change agents. These volunteers were, for the most part, social science majors in psychology or criminal justice. Students were committed to a three-term (year-long) involvement in the project and received course credit for their participation. Students were randomly selected from a large pool of those interested in project involvement and were randomly assigned to intervention conditions.

Procedure

Students in both experimental conditions received training in the techniques of behavioral contracting (Stuart, 1971) and child advocacy (Davidson and Rapp, 1976). Following training, students spent the remaining two terms providing services to referred youths. Youths were randomly matched to volunteers within condition, with the exception that male volunteers were not matched with female youths. Student volunteers were instructed to spend on the average of six to eight hours a week on their case. The actual duration of the intervention period was 18 school weeks or roughly five months.

The two intervention conditions differed in the following manner. Those students in the project condition continued to be supervised by graduate student project staff members following training. This condition mirrored the original model intervention procedures. Those in the court condition were supervised by a county court staff member following their training. In both instances, supervision sessions continued to meet in small groups. Students met on a weekly basis for two and a half hours during both training and supervision. This duration allowed ample time for individualized instruction and close supervision of intervention activity.

It was felt that the court condition represented an excellent example of a typical adopter setting with the added insight provided by the identically trained volunteer pool common to both experimental conditions. In that sense, intervention differences were anticipated to be due to a great extent to the differing political demands placed on the volunteers during implementation.

Measures

As noted earlier, the ideal implementation finds the student volunteer spending the bulk of the first several weeks in assessment-related activities and recreational activities. The major portion of the next several months is spent performing the advocacy and contracting activities outlined from the assessment interval. The final weeks are followed with the volunteer reducing his or her active involvement in the intervention process. The model is designed to provide proactive interventions in appropriate areas of the youths' life. However, as crises or additional contacts with the legal system occur, reactive steps are taken as is appropriate. Consequently, both the outcome and process measures were designed to monitor these very activities. Outcome measures were restricted to the assessment of whether or not the youths had had any formal contact with the juvenile authorities subsequent to their project referral. This was seen as a dichotomization of success versus failure. Thus, intervention patterns could be monitored such that different patterns of activities performed by volunteers with more successful cases could be differentiated from the patterns of activities performed with cases where youths had an additional contact with the system during project involvement.

The process measures were designed to assess the volunteers' adherence to the intervention model per se. Therefore, they served an important role in the evaluation of the impact of the court system on the intervention model. Each youth, one of his or her parents, and the undergraduate volunteer were interviewed at three equidistant points during the intervention interval. These process interviews attempted to gather information pertaining to the amount of time the volunteer spent in direct intervention-related activities, the amount of time the volunteer spent in recreational activities with the youth, the kinds of activities spent in school-related interventions, and the kinds of contracting activities implemented. Process scales were developed through a rational scale construction procedure, the success of which was then empirically evaluated (Jackson, 1971). The reliability and validity properties of these scales have been discussed elsewhere (Davidson, 1976; Kantrowitz et al., 1978; Blakely, 1981). These procedures produced internally consistent and relatively orthogonal scales.

RESULTS

Two of the 11 project condition youths recidivated during their formal involvement in the project (project failures). Of the 12 youths in the court condition, 6 had contact with the juvenile justice system subsequent to their referral to the project (court failures). Though the issues of outcome results is ultimately crucial to the evaluation of any program, in this instance the outcome issue is of primary concern in outlining the differential implementation patterns employed by volunteers in two conditions given the success or failure status of the youths during project involvement.

The scale assessing the average amount of time volunteers invested in their cases demonstrated that there were no significant condition differences. It was the case, however, that those volunteers working with youths who did not come into contact with the formal juvenile justice system (successes) spent more time on their cases than did those volunteers working with youths who got into further trouble during their involvement with the project ($F = 7.37, p < .02$).

However, the court successes tended to be involved in their intervention activities to a lesser extent than the court group failures or the project group successes or failures. In fact, the court failures tended to become much more active. In essence, it appears as if the court group volunteers were generally intervening in a much more reactive format than was initially intended by the model. That is, when the youths had an additional contact with the legal system, the volunteers were very reactive and intervened extensively. However, when the youths in the court condition did not have additional contacts with the legal system, the student volunteers were much less active.

The volunteers in the court group failures cell also showed considerably more intervention activity in the legal system per se than did volunteers in any of the other cells ($F = 6.13, p < .01$). This again conforms with the notion that volunteers in this group intervened in a reactive fashion.

A scale assessing interventions focused on modifying the school situation clearly demonstrated the recurrent pattern noted above. The highest activity level was noted in the court failure cell, while a drop was apparent in both the project successes and failures ($F = 4.14, p < .02$; see Table 7.1).

Several additional supportive findings were apparent in the recreational activities volunteers engaged in with their assigned youths. Volunteers in both cells of the court condition (successes and failures) tended to increase their recreational activity over time and were consistently higher than both project condition groups ($F = 9.07, p < .01$; see Table 7.2). Those volunteers involved in successful cases (no official contact with the police or court on the part of youth) generally tended to be more involved in recreational activities than did volunteers in unsuccessful cases ($F = 5.71, p < .05$). This disparity tended to increase over time in the project condition. However, due to the extremely high level of recreational activities in

TABLE 7.1   Mean Numbers of Interventions Focused on Modifying the School Situation

Experimental Conditions		Time Intervals		
		1	2	3
Project	Success	1.09	1.57	1.43
	Failure	1.73	1.09	1.00
Court	Success	1.57	1.36	2.00
	Failure	2.01	2.13	2.30

the court failure condition, this success/failure difference did not show up in the court condition.

The scale assessing contracting activities again showed the prominent pattern of high activity on the part of the court group failure (see Table 7.3). Though the overall main effects and interaction terms were not significant, several Scheffé comparisons did yield significant findings. The project condition successes showed a significant increase in contracting activities from Time 1 to Time 2 (F = 11.90, p < .01) and a nonsignificant drop to Time 3. The project condition failures showed a similar trend, though to a much lesser extent. The court condition successes increased their contracting activities over time, but not significantly. The court failures decreased their contracting over time.

DISCUSSION

The RD&D model calls for the implementation of criminal justice policy through a rational step-by-step process. Innovative social program ideas are evaluated and replicated through demonstration projects. Popular, successful demonstration projects receive national acclaim and are ultimately disseminated to potential users in applied settings. This data set suggests that the adopting organization can have a substantial impact on the disseminated criminal justice policy. In the project condition, the successes typically showed the greater amount of intervention activity (excluding reactive legal system involvement). The reverse was true of the court condition. Generally, the court condition failures showed a greater amount of intervention-related activities. This provides preliminary yet

TABLE 7.2   Mean Numbers of Recreational Activities

Experimental Conditions		Time Intervals		
		1	2	3
Project	Success	3.37	2.96	3.78
	Failure	2.67	1.50	1.34
Court	Success	3.67	3.70	4.00
	Failure	3.56	3.39	3.83

methodologically sound evidence that the host setting can dramatically affect program implementation.

The trends in the data showing the volunteers' recreational activities with the youth dramatically displayed the disparity between the conditions in terms of adherence to the intervention model (see Table 7.2). In general, the court condition volunteers spent a greater proportion of time in recreational activities than did the project condition volunteers. (Recall that the volunteers in the two conditions do not spend a different amount of total time in case-related activities.) Those in the project success cell showed a high level of recreational activity during the first third of the intervention period (Time 1), followed by a nearly significant drop to Time 2 and a significant rise again to Time 3 ($F = 10.81$, $p < .01$). This trend corresponds well with the intention of the model, as a good deal of recreational activity occurred during the assessment interval followed by a drop-off during the most critical intervention weeks and another rise in activity as the case moved toward termination. The project failures again showed the drop in recreational activity from Time 1 to Time 2 ($F = 4.89$, $p < .01$), but a drop continued on to termination (Time 3). This is perhaps due to the increased demands placed on these cases due to the additional contact with the legal system inherent in the failures.

The court group, on the other hand, showed a relatively stable pattern across both the success and failure cells; not only did the court condition volunteers spend a greater proportion of time in recreational activities, but they maintained this higher rate across time. The curves in Table 7.2 do not correspond to the trend theoretically anticipated given the specific nature of the intervention model.

The project success group clearly followed the expected pattern of moderate intervention activity during the first time interval, followed by an increase in activity at Time 2. Typically, the activity rate decreased to Time 3. These trends were evident in the school and contracting scales (see

TABLE 7.3   Mean Numbers of Contracting Intervention Activities

Experimental Conditions		Time Intervals		
		1	2	3
Project	Success	1.40	2.67	2.25
	Failure	1.26	1.33	1.22
Court	Success	1.23	1.47	1.99
	Failure	2.45	2.38	1.95

Tables 7.1 and 7.3) and corresponded well with the drop and subsequent rise in recreation-related activities. The project failures followed a similar pattern through the second time period; however, they frequently continued the increase in intervention-related activity through Time 3 and maintained a lower level of recreational activities. Again, this is probably related to the increased need to deal with the crisis situation and intervene in the appropriate areas on the youths' behalf.

These trends were not typically apparent in the court condition. The successes generally increased contracting activities over time right through the termination interval, when activities should have decreased (see Table 7.3). The failures showed the overall increased level of activity (see Table 7.3). One hypothesis that might explain the level of activity in the court failure cell lies in the tendency of court staff to focus the bulk of their attention on cases where there are current problems. Perhaps this is due to the oversized case loads that a typical probation officer must endure. In any case, it is apparent that this increased activity level was related to the differential supervision that existed in the court group. The court failures tended to spend a little more time on their cases and were somewhat more recreationally oriented (see Table 7.2). They were also more likely to be involved in specific contracting related activities than were the court successes (see Table 7.3).

In interpreting these findings it is crucial to recall the differences in the intervention conditions. The volunteers were all trained by project staff in the same skills using the same materials. Both the youths and volunteers were randomly matched and were randomly assigned to intervention conditions. Following the training, half of the volunteers were supervised by court staff. The remaining half were supervised by project staff. They all came from the same pool and intervened in the same community settings and at the same time. Yet, differential intervention activities were consistently noted across several process scales designed specifically to monitor the intervention process across time. The issue here is what components of the innovation the court group adopted. The volunteers did implement the intervention strategies to some extent. What they failed to do was maintain an investment in the philosophy of the diversion model. They continued to petition youth to the juvenile court. In short, diversion was not their business. Though they practiced some of the project intervention strategies, there was little or no systemic impact apparent at the court. If we cannot produce similar results in a dissemination effort this minimally removed from the original innovation, it is questionable that dissemination efforts through traditional workshops across the country will have any greater hope in producing adopters that incorporate the essential ingredients of the innovation within the daily operating structure of their organizations.

In summary, dissemination research has typically focused on the strategies of persuading organizations to adopt the innovation. The fact that this objective can be accomplished given the requisite amount of effort has frequently been addressed in the literature (Fairweather, 1967; Fairweather et al., 1974). However, it is apparent that this is an insufficient step in the overall model. Observers are increasingly questioning the return on the federal investment in research and development in the social sciences. The issue of the effectiveness of this dissemination model, both in terms of the degree to which the innovation is implemented by adopting organizations and in terms of outcome data at the level of adopting organizations, is just now beginning to receive its due attention (Emshoff et al., 1980).

However, accompanying this observation is the overwhelming awareness of the lack of rigorous research on how to ensure the most efficient utilization of social innovations. Increased attention must be paid to the manner in which adopting organizations reinvent the innovation as it is adapted to the demands of their organizational structure. Though the current research has taken but a small step in the direction of pinpointing the extent of this problem, it has clearly suggested the presence of a substantial problem inherent in the implementation phase of the current demonstration project model of disseminating criminal justice policy.

REFERENCES

BERMAN, P. and M. McLAUGHLIN (1978) Federal Programs Supporting Educational Change, Vol. VIII: Implementing and Sustaining Innovations. Santa Monica, CA: Rand.

BLAKELY, C. H. (1981) "The diversion of juvenile delinquents: a first step toward the dissemination of a successful innovation." Ph.D. dissertation, Michigan State University.

CHARTERS, W. W. and J. E. JONES (1973) "On the risks of appraising nonevents in program evaluation." Educ. Researcher 2: 5-7.

DAVIDSON, W. S. (1976) "The diversion of juvenile offenders: a comparison of the process and relative efficacy of behavioral contracting and child advocacy." Ph.D. dissertation, University of Illinois.

——— and C. A. RAPP (1976) "Child advocacy in the justice system." Social Work 21: 225-232.

DAVIDSON, W. S., E. SEIDMAN, J. RAPPAPORT, P. BERCK, N. RAPP, W. RHODES, and J. HERRING (1977) "Diversion program for juvenile offenders." Social Work Research and Abstracts 13: 40-49.

EMSHOFF, J. G., W. S. DAVIDSON, N. SCHMITT, and N. LEEDOM (1980) "Salient processes in the implementation of social technology." Grant proposal funded by the National Science Foundation.

EVELAND, J. D., E. M. ROGERS, and C. KLEPPER (1977) "The innovation process in public organizations: some elements of a preliminary model." Final report. Grant #RDS-7517952, National Science Foundation. University of Michigan.

FAIRWEATHER, G. W. (1967) Methods for Experimental Social Innovation. New York: John Wiley.

——— D. H. SANDERS, and L. G. TORNATZKY (1974) Creating Change in Mental Health Organizations. New York: Pergamon.

HAVELOCK, R. (1969) Planning for Innovation through Dissemination and Utilization of Knowledge. Ann Arbor, MI: Institute for Social Research.

HOUSE, E. R. (1981) "Three perspectives on innovations: technological, political, and cultural," pp. 17-41 in R. Lehming and M. Kane (eds.) Improving Schools: Using What We Know. Beverly Hills, CA: Sage.

JACKSON, D. N. (1971) "A sequential strategy for personality scale development," pp. 61-94 in C. Spielberger (ed.) Issues in Clinical and Community Psychology. New York: Academic Press.

KANTROWITZ, R. E., W. S. DAVIDSON, C. H. BLAKELY, and M. G. KUSHLER (1978) "The effect of training/supervision on nonprofessional interventions with delinquents." Presented at the 86th Annual Convention of the American Psychological Association, Toronto.

RAPPAPORT, J., E. SEIDMAN, and W. S. DAVIDSON (1979) "Before the beginning and after the end," pp. 109-144 in L. Snowden, R. Munoz, and J. Kelly (eds.) Research in Social Contexts: Bringing About Change. San Francisco: Jossey-Bass.

STUART, R. B. (1971) "Behavioral contracting within the families of delinquents." J. of Behavior Therapy and Experimental Psychiatry 2: 1-11.

WILLIAMS, W. (1976) "Implementation analysis and assessment," pp. 267-292 in W. Williams and R. Elmore (eds.) Social Program Implementation. New York: Academic Press.

8

Scott H. Decker

University of Missouri-St. Louis

VALUE CONSENSUS AMONG AGENCIES
IN A JUVENILE DIVERSION PROGRAM
A Process Evaluation

The coordination of agencies involved in the pursuit of similar goals is an important theoretical, empirical, and practical issue. Seldom is it the case that a single public sector agency is the exclusive group in pursuit of some objective. Education, transportation, mental health, and criminal justice are all examples of tax-supported ventures pursued by confederations of agencies. The degree of interdependence among those groups will have an important bearing on the identification of legitimate goals as well as the achievement of those goals. These confederations are characterized by the lack of a centralized authority. The lack of centralization can have important consequences for the ability of agencies within the confederation to cooperate and ultimately achieve collective goals. Critical to this process is the set of values held by the participants about appropriate ends and functions. Clearly, values and attitudes may be much more diffuse in decentralized environments, and such value divergence can inhibit if not totally prevent the achievement of goals.

This problem is particularly relevant for relatively new programs. Innovations in social policy frequently call for the alignment of groups that lack a history of informal or formal interaction. Thus considerable role and value definition must occur for effective pursuit of stated objectives. The failure to achieve some level of consensus regarding appropriate strategies of action, patterns of interagency interaction, means of resolving "trouble cases," and division of labor will have serious consequences for the success of the venture. Attitudinal conflict is a greater likelihood for efforts that are not highly technological. Thus programs lacking formalized techniques for task completion are likely to encounter more difficulties in this regard. Counseling settings are a good example of low-technology situations that may produce conflict about the appropriate targets for action and techniques for intervention.

It was noted earlier that criminal justice involved the confederated efforts of a variety of public sector agencies. In many respects the concept of exchange in analyzing interorganizational relations is most appropriately suited to the study of crime control efforts (Cole, 1973). Clearly, the absence of a centralized authority diminishes the chances of attitudinal consensus and enhances negotiations between agencies. The recent "explosion" in police diversion programs (Klein et al., 1976) provides an appropriate setting in which the degree of value consensus among the primary agencies involved in such efforts can be assessed. Traditionally isolated groups (especially police and treatment personnel) have been drawn together in the effort to prevent penetration of juvenile offenders into the juvenile justice system. The success of such programs depends on the coordination of effort between the police (who act as the primary referral agent) and treatment personnel (who provide postreferral services). Because such efforts involve two groups not constrained by an objective or technological directive, considerable divergence of goals and techniques exists. Thus, therapeutic and punitive strategies can be recommended in the same situation by each group. Although such programs have received extensive review and analysis in the literature, there has been no examination of the extent to which values between the two groups are similar. The current analysis provides an empirical examination of this important issue.

REVIEW OF THE LITERATURE

While there have been frequent examinations of attitudes of criminal justice personnel, few have focused on the attitudes and values in a specific program. In a test of the proposition that treatment and police agents differ attitudinally, Gottfredson and Gottfredson (1969) examined police and probation officers' attitudes toward juvenile detention. They found differences between the groups on two factors: societal protection and child protection. Police scored higher than probation officers on the first factor, and in the vignettes presented were more likely to dispose of cases by using detention than were the probation personnel. Wheeler et al. (1968) examined frequency of contacts and similarity of attitudes among seven groups actively involved in delinquency control. Substantial differences existed between police agents (police chiefs and Juvenile Bureau Officers) and those with a treatment mandate (probation officers, psychiatrists, social workers, and school guidance counselors). The authors underscored the considerable "probems of integration and communication" (1968: 42) likely to result from such distance. They also noted that conflicts may be faced by probation officers, since they have the greatest contact with police and judges, groups that rate distant from them in attitude.

Up to this point I have focused on attitudinal differences between treatment personnel and police in general. The existence of such differences was not surprising. But it may well be the case that such a cleavage would not be found within the context of a specific program. That is, perhaps a common pursuit involving the two groups would produce greater similarity of attitudes. Certainly that is not an unreasonable proposition. There is already considerable evidence that the police are required to fulfill a variety of roles in the community, some of which are social service or treatment oriented (Bard and Berkowitz, 1967; Reiss, 1972; Cumming et al., 1965). Therefore it seems reasonable that a program with clearly articulated goals and well-defined roles may be able to reduce the disparity in attitudes. The results of such attitudinal convergence, it is hoped, could be the more effective disposition of duties by each group and an increased level of goal achievement.

Bard and Berkowitz (1969) did find it possible to integrate police and mental health personnel successfully. After a period of training they found police could successfully incorporate social work and psychotherapeutic skills into their role. A more extensive analysis was conducted by Treger et al. (1974) in conjunction with a treatment program involving police and social workers. Its goals were similar to those of most diversion programs: to provide (1) social work assessments of clients, (2) 24-hour crisis intervention, (3) short- and long-term counseling, and (4) referral to community agencies. Initial police attitudes toward social work were negative, and most police indicated that they had little contact with or knowledge of the role of social workers. Correspondingly, few of the social workers involved in the program had positive attitudes about the police. Treger et al. reported that shortly after the inception of the program a reversal of these attitudes occurred for each group. The ultimate success of the program was traced to the ability of the two groups to cooperate and achieve a common understanding. While the methodology used in producing these findings is not fully reported (i.e., the absence of a baseline measurement, no description of measurement devices, no presentation of difference or change scores), cooperation was reported as an important element for the success of the program.

Diversion programs seem an appropriate setting in which to examine the attitudinal differences between police and treatment personnel. The exchange framework is particularly relevant to understanding diversion. In the network of juvenile justice the police act as the primary agent of referral through which youths to be processed usually pass. Police control the important decision about *where* a youth will be referred. Thus agreement with the goals of diversion as well as some similarity in attitude with those who provide services to diverted youth are essential to program success. In the absence of such agreement, several negative consequences may result. First, police may not agree with the goals of diversion and either "dump" trouble cases into such programs or make so few referrals as to effectively produce the demise of the program. Second, another alternative may be an excessive number of referrals to such programs due to a lack of understanding about diversion. In the absence of police support for diversionary goals and some level of attitudinal agreement with treatment staff, successful program operation is unlikely. Because the police serve as the "gatekeeper" to the counseling (or service) stage of the diversion process, they may doom the program by providing too many, too few, or wholly inappropriate referrals.

There are some indications that important attitudinal differences exist between the groups involved in diversion programs. Specifically, police and treatment groups have been identified as possessing varying, and sometimes conflicting, views regarding the appropriate disposition of minor offenders. The preceding section of this chapter has identified differences in attitudes between enforcement and treatment personnel in general. Such differences seem to apply to the specific practice of diversion. Klein (1976a) indicates that there has been police resistance to diversion programs. He specifically notes that several police interviews indicated that such efforts were either "inappropriate" or "defeated enforcement goals" (1976a: 422). He speculates that there has apparently been some change in that orientation. He also states that juvenile matters generally are assigned a low priority and that diversion ranks low even within that status. Klein (1976b) provides further support for the contention that diversion programs lack police support in noting that many police officers view diversion as opposed to legitimate police goals.

Many police officers decry diversion practices—especially diversion without referral as being antithetical to police goals and of no rehabilitative value. In fact, it is often suggested that to release youngsters without further action is tantamount to *rewarding* them or showing them that they can get away with their legal transgressions [Klein, 1976b: 79].

In addition to this evidence, Klein et al. (1976) indicate that where diversion programs have been implemented it is often the case that only a minority of officers participate in the program by providing referrals.

DATA SOURCES

Data for the current analysis were drawn from the third (final) year of a federally funded diversion program for status offenders (The Status Offender Service Unit) in the city of St. Louis. The program staff consists of a director and five full-time deputy juvenile officers. Of the 754 referrals received between January 1, 1980 and October 30, 1980, 75 percent were provided by the police, with the remainder being referred by the family. Only residents of the City of St. Louis under 17 with no more than one prior minor referral to the juvenile court were eligible for program selection. Upon referral, the parents of the juvenile are contacted by the director and an initial appointment with a deputy juvenile officer is recommended. Program participation from then on is voluntary. Following the initial appointment several options exist: (1) The case may be closed based on the decision that no further services are necessary; (2) the juvenile may be referred to the juvenile court; (3) short-term counseling may take place within the Status Offender Service Unit (SOSU); or (4) the client may be referred to one of the 15 agencies contracted to provide specialized counseling services. Each of these contract agencies had an individual assigned to serve as a liaison with the SOSU.

The treatment personnel group in this analysis comprises all six members of SOSU plus the liaison person (who was also actively involved in providing treatment to referral juveniles) from each of the 15 contracted agencies. Thus the treatment respondents represent a group of individuals knowledgeable of and actively involved in the diversion program.

Though they may play somewhat different roles in the diversion process, each is involved in a postreferral, treatment capacity. Thus a commonality of function exists for them as a group. The Juvenile Police Officer results represent 45 of the 53 members of the Juvenile Bureau of the St. Louis Metropolitan Police Department. These officers are assigned to nine districts with frequent rotations. Since few, if any, police referrals were provided by regular patrol officers (i.e., non-Juvenile Division offi-

TABLE 8.1   Frequency of Contact with Related Agencies[a]

	Juvenile Police Officers (n = 45)			Treatment Staff (n = 21)		
	rank	$\overline{x}$	s	rank	$\overline{x}$	s
1. Juvenile Court Judges	7	5.9	2.2	7	7.3	1.7
2. School Officials	4	4.2	2.2	4	4.9	2.0
3. Diversion Program Director	6	5.3	2.4	6	6.2	1.8
4. Diversion Program Staff	5	4.9	2.2	3	3.7	1.8
5. Police Officers	1	2.4	2.1	1	1.6	1.2
6. Parents of Referrals	2	2.8	2.1	2	2.5	1.2
7. Juvenile Police Officers	3	3.4	2.2	5	5.8	2.0

[a] Responses to the question, "Please assign a number to each of the following agencies indicating how frequently you have had contact with it due *directly* to the Diversion Program. An 8 indicates the fewest contacts, and a 1 the most."

cers), the Juvenile Police Officers represent those most actively involved in the referral phase of the program.

RESULTS

It is important to determine what patterns of contact and convergence of attitude exist for the police and treatment groups. Support for the goals of diversion among the groups is essential to both the smooth operation of the mechanics of referral and treatment and ultimately the achievement of program objectives.

Frequency of contact with related agencies or groups due directly to the program is presented in Table 8.1. The mean rankings for the police group indicate that the category "other police officers" was ranked first. It is interesting to note that the group listed second was the parents of referrals. It cannot be determined if such a pattern of contact between juvenile officers and parents would exist independent of the program. But it seems important that this group be singled out, indicating that police decisions are not being made without contact with a group important to the diversion process, the parents of referrals. Other Juvenile Police Officers were ranked third, perhaps indicating something about the relatively small number of such officers and the isolated nature of their work. Though no formal role existed within the SOSU diversion framework for school personnel, they represent an important contact for Juvenile Police, and indeed were ranked higher than either the SOSU staff or director. The lowest ranking, indicating least frequent contact, was for juvenile court judges. As would be expected, this illustrates that police have more contact with agencies at the initial stages of the juvenile justice system. Stated differently, the further one penetrates into the system, the less likely it is that police will have much contact with that segment of the system. This may have positive consequences for the establishment of relations with others at the "front end" of the system, such as persons involved in diversion. If frequent contacts are an important element in the creation of a working consensus among agencies, this seems a significant point. To the extent that the goals of the juvenile justice system are somewhat different at the stages of referral, intake, and adjustment, this finding seems especially important.

Table 8.1 also presents the rankings by the treatment staff. All but two of the rankings were the same as for the police. Treatment personnel ranked police officers as the group they had contact with most frequently. This may be due to the inappropriate referrals made by this group that led to contacts or the failure of the treatment staff to differentiate accurately between police officers and Juvenile Police Officers on the questionnaire. Parents of referrals received the second ranking, as was the case for the Juvenile Police Officers. The only differences in rankings occurred for the positioning of diversion program staff and juvenile police officers. The treatment staff ranked them as third and fifth, respectively, the reverse of the police rankings. These differences highlight the point made earlier: that interactions occur more frequently among agencies with similar functions. Thus the treatment staff ranks diversion program staff (SOSU personnel) higher than did the police respondents.

A related issue is examined in Table 8.2, which depicts perceived similarity of attitude toward status offenders. Each of the two groups was asked to rank order seven related agencies according to how similar its attitude was about status offenders to their own. It is interesting that Diversion Program Staff were ranked as nearer in attitude (second) than police officers (third), although by a close margin. Social workers received the fourth (middle ranking) from police. This is inconsistent with the findings reported in the literature review and suggests somewhat of a treatment orientation among juvenile officers. Clergy and school officials each received the fifth ranking, while juvenile court judges were ranked as most distant in attitude.

The treatment staff ranked police officers as holding attitudes about status offenders most similar to their own. This result was unexpected because of the treatment enforcement antagonisms identified in the litera-

TABLE 8.2   Similarity of Attitude to Related Agencies[a]

	Juvenile Police Officers (n = 45)			Treatment Staff (n = 21)		
	rank	$\overline{x}$	s	rank	$\overline{x}$	s
1. Juvenile Court Judges	7	4.2	2.5	6	5.1	2.0
2. School Officials	5	3.9	2.3	5	3.9	1.9
3. Diversion Program Staff	2	3.0	2.4	4	3.5	1.8
4. Police Officers	3	3.1	2.4	1	1.4	0.7
5. Juvenile Police Officers	1	2.0	1.8	3	3.4	1.8
6. Social Workers	4	3.7	2.1	2	2.6	1.2
7. Clergy	5	3.9	2.1	7	5.6	1.7

[a] Responses to the question, "Please assign a number to each of the following agencies or people indicating how similar their attitudes about status offenders are to your own. A 7 indicates the greatest difference and a 1 the most similarity."

ture. Several suggestions are offered in this context. Either exceptional relationships between the treatment group and the police have developed, or the treatment personnel hold mistaken notions about police attitudes. Another interpretation of this result may be found in the relative absence of contact between these two groups. Police officers traditionally attempt to minimize their contact with all but the most serious juvenile offenders. Because such officers would have little contact with less serious offenders, their attitudes would tend to be more positive. Social workers received the second ranking, not altogether unexpected given the social work background possessed by many of the treatment staff. Juvenile Police Officers (third) and diversion program staff (fourth) received similar mean rankings by the treatment staff. Juvenile court judges and clergy were seen as having the two least similar attitudes.

Five specific concerns are addressed in Table 8.3. Four of the issues raised were considered vital to the successful operation of the program; the fifth is of general interest. In the absence of agreement about these values, the cooperation of the two groups most vital to the diversionary process would be lacking. The four attitudinal dimensions related to diversion include the appropriate agency to handle status offenders, the elimination of status offenses, the worthiness of diversion, and the perceived effectiveness of the SOSU program. The final issue is that of punishment and desert for juveniles.

The growth of diversion programs has been tied to the labeling perspective. As such, a stated programmatic emphasis has been placed on reducing

TABLE 8.3   Summary of Differences Between Police and Treatment
Groups' Attitudes Toward Diversion[a]

Question	Police $\overline{x}$	Treatment $\overline{x}$	t value	df	Probability (one-tailed)
1. I would prefer another agency than the police to handle status offenders.	3.53	3.85	.87	64	N.S.
2. Status offenses should be eliminated	1.91	2.38	1.51	64	N.S.
3. The concept of diverting status offenders from the juvenile court is a worthwhile objective.	4.20	4.29	.33	64	N.S.
4. Programs like the Status Offender Service Unit don't have much effect on delinquency.	2.14	1.71	2.50	63	.01
5. One of the problems with the juvenile justice system is that most kids don't get the punishment they deserve.	3.51	2.14	5.03	64	<.0005

[a] Responses are based on a five-point Likert scale, with 5 = strongly agree, 4 = agree, 3 = neutral, 2 = disagree, 1 = strongly disagree.

the presumably stigmatizing consequences of contact with formal agencies. Certainly the police represent one of the important agencies in this process. One potential means of reducing stigma, therefore, would be to place a different group in the role of referral agent. Indeed, throughout the operation of the program the police frequently expressed the opinion that status offenders took up valuable police time that could better be spent in other ways. The first question in Table 8.3 allows us to assess the degree of agreement for the two groups with the notion that another agency should handle status offenders. Both groups tend to agree that an agency other than the police would be preferable. Though treatment personnel were slightly inclined to favor an alternative to the police (3.85 to 3.53), the differences did not approach statistical significance. It appears that the two groups favor some alternative to that of the police being the primary agency to handle status offenders. Current realities dictate (and likely will continue to do so) that the police serve as the primary agent of referral for status offenders. The proximity of attitude indicates that this issue is not one that differentiates well between the two groups. Thus on this first matter there is consensus.

A number of groups (among them the National Council on Crime and Delinquency and the President's Advisory Commission on Criminal Justice Standards and Goals) have called for the elimination of status offenses from juvenile codes. Neither the juvenile police officers or the treatment personnel are in agreement with these efforts. It is interesting to observe that the mean for the police ($\bar{x}$ = 1.91) is lower than that for the treatment group ($\bar{x}$ = 2.38) in light of the fact that a portion of the latter are directly dependent on the existence of a class of status offenders for employment. Though the police cited numerous difficulties in handling that category of juveniles, they appear to favor the continued use of the legal category of misconduct. The differences between the two groups (measured by a t-test) again failed to attain statistical significance. Thus agreement with the existence of status offenses is not an issue that successfully allows us to differentiate between police and treatment personnel, indicating consensus about an issue of importance to the operation of the program.

Perhaps the most essential point of agreement among agencies in a confederation is consensus about the concepts that underlie the program. Klein (1976b) has identified police opposition to diversion programs. It is easy to locate the source of such opposition. If one of the duties of the police is to identify law-violating behavior and take the responsible individuals into custody, it is readily apparent that diversion contradicts this practice. It seems that the release of identified law violators to a nonpunitive outlet would deliberately frustrate an important police mandate. In order for such programs to operate effectively it must be demonstrated that the concept of diverting status offenders from the juvenile court receives support from the police. This is the third issue examined in Table 8.3. The mean levels of agreement for the police and the treatment group are very close: 4.20 and 4.29, respectively. It appears from these values that both groups expressed strong support for the most primary of issues to a diversion project. The lack of police participation reported by Klein et al. (1976) is not explicable by opposition to the concept of diversion itself. The t-test failed to identify a significant difference between the two groups, and therefore it provides strong support for the concept of diversion.

In addition to support for the concept of diversion, belief in the efficacy of the program is necessary for continued program participation and commitment to goals. Agencies and individuals who support the goals of a program but believe that it does not work are likely to become cynical and reduce their level of participation and ultimately their support for the program. Both the police and treatment groups disagree with the statement that the program did not have much effect on delinquency. The treatment personnel felt more strongly that the program had an effect, however. This finding adds to those noted for the preceding three issues. For each, police and treatment agency personnel expressed similar attitudes—attitudes which indicated support for the diversion program. A significant difference between police and treatment personnel was not found for the first three issues. Such a difference did emerge with regard to the perceived effect of the program. The difference between the two was significant at the .01 level, with treatment personnel feeling more strongly about the positive effect of the program.

The final issue examined is a general one, not specifically related to diversion. It is concerned with the perception about punishment received by most juveniles. Specifically, we are concerned with documenting the extent to which the two groups believe that juveniles do not get the punishment they deserve from the criminal justice system. The preceding literature review indicated that police maintained a more punitive orientation than groups in the criminal justice system involved in the provision of treatment services. Indeed, some police opposition to the concept of diversion indicated by Klein (1976b) and Klein et al. (1976) may well be due to the contention that such practices circumvent the punishment due many juveniles. Certainly police are more familiar with a broader spectrum of juvenile misbehavior than treatment personnel. Though the referral of a juvenile in a particular instance may be for a minor issue of wrongdoing, the officer may have knowledge of either previous or more serious law-violating behavior. The inclusion of this general issue allows a more specific inference to be drawn about the differences between the two groups with respect to the diversionary process. If it is true that police and treatment groups' attitudes are consistent with respect to diversionary concepts, but do differ on a broader topic, a case can be made that despite some attitudinal gaps, agency cooperation appears feasible.

The fifth comparison in Table 8.3 examines this issue. The mean level of agreement for the juvenile officers was 3.51, indicating moderate agreement that juveniles do not receive the punishment they deserve. Those involved in treatment, however, tended to disagree with the statement ($\bar{x}$ = 2.14). This topic represents the first clear juxtaposition of attitudes. It is the first on which the two groups have disagreed, and displays the greatest magnitude of difference between the two means. The null hypothesis can clearly be rejected (t = 5.03, df = 64, p ≤ .0005), indicating a significant difference between the attitudes of the two groups on this issue. It is apparent, then, that while Juvenile Police Officers and those involved in providing treatment services share similar attitudes regarding diversion and status offenders, they disagree about a more general concern. Values, goals, and effect of the program were viewed uniformly, which indicates that the foundation for smooth and efficient program operation was present.

DISCUSSION AND CONCLUSION

I have examined an issue that has received little attention in the program evaluation literature: the extent and role of value consensus among agencies. It was suggested that the degree of interdependence among the involved agencies was an ingredient important to the development of effective interagency linkages. This issue is particularly critical in a criminal justice setting, where relationships exist within a decentralized setting, where linkages depend on less formal elements. One of the ways in which this issue can be most readily assessed is through examination of the frequency of contact and attitudinal perceptions of groups involved in the delivery of services to clients. Groups with frequent contacts may be expected to create a working consensus or compromise about program functions. Agencies with similar attitudes toward other program participants may find integration of functions nonproblematic. Those groups that lack contact with each other or perceive themselves to be attitudinally isolated from a service network may have difficulty forging vital linkages with other agencies. An additional element to the formation of such ties is the extent to which the program's goals and operations are valued. Groups that reject the legitimacy of a program, see it as contradictory to higher-order goals, or, worse, perceive it to be ineffective are unlikely to participate in a significant fashion. In addition, when significant differences between primary program participants exist about these issues, the exchange process will be blunted.

This set of organizational concerns was examined within the context of a diversion program for status offenders. Two specific groups were chosen for analysis as the primary program participants: juvenile police officers and treatment personnel involved in counseling and related services. Taken together, those two groups comprise the most significant sources of referral and disposition. As such, the exchange process between them was critical to program operation. Minor differences existed in the frequency of contacts with related agencies. Only two of seven related agencies received a different rank from the two groups. Attitudes toward those agencies showed much greater differences, however. Treatment personnel saw their attitudes about status offenders as most consistent with those of police officers and social workers, while juvenile police officers ranked other juvenile officers and the diversion program staff first and second, respectively. This suggests there is no clear or consistent pattern of rankings that can differentiate the two groups.

When four topics related to diversion, status offenders, and the program were analyzed, a consistent pattern did emerge. There was considerable agreement among the groups on all four issues. Only one significant difference was observed, for perceptions of the effectiveness of the program. While both Juvenile Police Officers and the treatment group agreed that the program was not ineffective, the treatment group, as expected, felt more strongly about its effect. A fifth comparison provided an exception to this. Despite the agreement noted above, a considerable difference was found on the issue of punishment. The police found themselves more likely to agree that juveniles failed to receive the punishment they deserved, while the treatment personnel expressed a different perspective. Perhaps the overall pattern of agreement suggests that the expected discrepancies between the two groups was mistaken. These results appear to lend support to the "expansion of control" hypothesis, in that the police support diversion and favor punishment.

The police maintained a (more) punitive orientation even in the midst of their participation in a diversion program. Because they perceive a problem with the juvenile justice system to be a lack of punishment, police may view diversion programs as an appropriate way to ensure that "justice" is done. Rather than diverting juveniles who would have been processed in the absence of diversion programs, they refer a new population to such programs. By maintaining a level of formal referrals equal to that before diversion, such programs allow the police to introduce a substantially new population to the juvenile justice system.

One of the key elements to successful program operation is the linkages between agencies. In the absence of carefully controlled experiments or reasonable approximations thereof (quasi-experimental designs), process evaluations can provide valuable information to agencies about one aspect of program function—values regarding program operation.

REFERENCES

BARD, M. and B. BERKOWITZ (1967) "Training police as specialists in family crisis intervention: a community psychology action program" Community Mental Health J. 13: 315-317.

BARD, M. and B. BERKOWITZ (1969) "A community psychology consultation program in police and family crisis intervention." Int. J. of Social Psychiatry 15: 209-215.

COLE, G. (1973) Politics and the Administration of Justice. Beverly Hills, CA: Sage.

CUMMING, E., I. CUMMING and L. EDELL (1965) "Policeman as philosopher, guide and friend." Social Problems 12: 276-286.

GOTTFREDSON, D. and G. GOTTFREDSON (1969) "Decision-maker attitudes and juvenile detention." Research in Crime and Delinquency 6: 177-198.

KLEIN, M. (1976a) "Issues and realities in police diversion programs." Crime and Delinquency 22: 421-427.

——— (1976b) "Issues in police diversion of juvenile offenders," pp. 73-104 in R. M. Carter and M. W. Klein (eds.) Back on the Street. Englewood Cliffs, NJ: Prentice-Hall.

KLEIN, M. W., K. S. TEILMANN, J. A. STYLES, S. B. LINCOLN, and S. LABIN-ROSENWEIG (1976) "The explosion in police diversion programs: evaluating the structural dimensions of a social fad," pp. 101-120 in M. W. Klein (ed.) The Juvenile Justice System. Beverly Hills, CA: Sage.

REISS, A. (1972) The Police and the Public. New Haven: Yale Univ. Press.

TREGER, H., D. THOMSON, and G. JAECK (1974) "A police-social work team model: some preliminary findings and implications for system change." Crime and Delinquency 20: 281-290.

WHEELER, S., E. BONACICH, M. R. CRAMER, and I. K. ZOLA (1968) "Agents of delinquency control: a comparative analysis," pp. 31-60 in S. Wheeler (ed.) Controlling Delinquents. New York: John Wiley.

9

C. Ronald Huff

Ohio State University

Geoffrey P. Alpert

University of Miami

ORGANIZATIONAL COMPLIANCE WITH COURT-ORDERED REFORM
The Need for Evaluation Research

During the past two decades, courts have played an increasingly significant role in regulating behavior and serving as an impetus for social change. Courts, as social institutions, have as their major charge the protection of an individual or group from being injured by another. In practice, however, the courts provide a forum where disputes—whether civil, criminal, or administrative—can be resolved fairly and justly. Today hardly any aspect of daily life remains untouched by courts in their role as social control agents. The court structure is complex and often confusing; different courts have different mandates, jurisdictions, and power (Rubin, 1976). Although the general principles and overall implications of court decisions, opinions, and orders may be extended to such institutional settings as schools, mental hospitals, and other components of governmentally directed services, the focus of this chapter will be on correctional institutions and their compliance with court orders.[1]

We often read that some federal district court has issued a decree calling for "sweeping reforms" of a prison or an entire prison system. Headlines call to our attention the fact that a judicial decision has been reached and that the defendants will be "forced to comply." But do they? What really happens once the decision has been written, reported, and duly dissem-

115

inated? It turns out that we know very little about this process that has been called institutional reform, and specifically we know very little about decree implementation as a means of reform (Willie and Greenblatt, 1981).

Extant studies (see, for example, Note, 1981; Nathan, 1979; Harvard Center for Criminal Justice, 1972; Haas and Champagne, 1976; Becker and Feeley, 1975; Wasby, 1970; Krislov, 1972; Katz, 1965; Miller, 1965; Thomas, 1980; Alexander, 1978; Harris and Spiller, 1977) generally provide descriptions of the problems inherent in the implementation process and document the need for in-depth case studies to determine the dynamics of this implementation process and to identify the nature of the problems so that implementation might be improved. There also exists limited but valuable case study material on specific examples of the implementation process in criminal justice. However, until we have a larger sample of such cases, it will be difficult to formulate a general theory of decree implementation and its impact on social institutions. What is the real utility of formal legal decisions as a means of social reform? Indeed, it has been argued (Thomas, 1980) that the complexity of the issues and the current state of knowledge concerning the implementation of legal reform have combined to render impotent the reform potential of correctional law. To illustrate the issues and problems surrounding implementation and related research on institutional reform, our discussion will focus on correctional law and, specifically, prison reform.

EVOLUTION OF PRISONERS' RIGHTS:
HOW REAL?

Not so long ago, we lacked a jurisprudence of penology; and in fact, correctional law today is far from fully developed. Nevertheless, the courts' views of prisoners have evolved through a number of stages, though not by any means in a linear progression. From the view that prisoners were really "slaves of the state" and without rights (Ruffin v. Virginia, 1871), over time the courts have postulated the following views: (1) that prisoners are presumed to retain the usual rights of all citizens unless the state can demonstrate a compelling interest in restricting such rights (Coffin v. Reichard, 1944); (2) that prisoners forfeit the usual rights granted to citizens unless they can show why they should have these rights (Price v. Johnston, 1948); and (3) that the courts should keep their hands off the administration of prisons (Banning v. Looney, 1954). The present era is one of conflicting judicial messages, with the federal district courts issuing decisions much more liberal and progressive than the U.S. Supreme

Court, whose earlier decisions actually serve as the basis for the current federal court decrees. And to make matters even more complicated, we see inconsistencies in the views of the high court which confuse not only the federal district courts but public officials charged with administering, managing, and policy making.[2]

Now that constitutional and statutory rights have in theory been extended inside the prison gates, the question becomes whether those rights are really enforced on a day-to-day basis. Or, in the absence of such a high level of implementation, are these rights *generally* available to prisoners? Probably the most accurate answer is that we don't really know and it is very hard to find out.

THE IMPLEMENTATION OF JUDICIAL DECREES

Unlike the field of education, which has a rich history of judicial intervention (Willie and Greenblatt, 1981), questions concerning court orders and judicial decrees in correctional settings remain unanswered. This is not to suggest that no research has been conducted. On the contrary, some excellent case studies, survey research, and other inquiries have produced some tentative findings and researchable hypotheses. More and better research must be conducted, however, before we can discuss middle-range theories of implementation or compliance. A major problem is that the field from which to select relevant cases (those decided in the plaintiff's favor and which include broad issues and have a variety of enforcement mechanisms) is quite small.

The research that has been conducted is most helpful in evaluating the state of the art, and the following discussion will highlight the most significant contributions.

One of the first studies of the impact of judicial decrees in corrections was conducted by the Harvard Center for Criminal Justice (1972). This group examined the consent decree issued by the court in Morris v. Travisono (1970) and the court's effectiveness as an institutional mechanism to assure fairness of implementation. The essence of their conclusion was that "courts would not seem particularly well-suited for such a task" (1972: 227). Subsequently, a more sophisticated study, using four correctional law cases, permitted a complex comparative analysis (Harris and Spiller, 1977). These researchers reviewed numerous variables which had, at least theoretically, an impact on compliance and several methods to ensure compliance. Finally, Nathan (1979) published a key article on the use of court-appointed "masters" in institutional reform and provided the reader (and the courts) with a number of viable alternatives to ensure compliance. Nathan advocates the use of masters, monitors, ombudsmen, and human rights committees to effect decree implementation. Depending on the particular situation and issues, these enforcers can have a positive impact.

SOME UNANSWERED QUESTIONS

We have identified several areas of inquiry which need to be addressed before a theoretical model of implementation can be developed. The following illustrative questions, while not exhausting the issues, indicate at least part of the research agenda.

(1) What factors contribute to compliance or noncompliance with court-ordered reform?
(2) What are the unanticipated consequences of such reform within the organizational context?
(3) What impact does court-ordered reform have on the employees, the management, and the clients (in this case, prisoners *and* the public)?
(4) What strategies are used by organizations to facilitate or to impede compliance?

There exists a limited body of research findings related to these issues. We know, for example, that the presence of a "friendly defendent" does not necessarily ensure that successful implementation will occur. On the contrary, the existence of conflict between the court and the defendant has more often been associated with eventual implementation of the decree. We also know that judicial activism in initiating deadlines, and other attempts to enforce compliance, appears to be associated with increased compliance behavior (Harris and Spiller, 1977).

These kinds of preliminary findings, based on relatively detailed but numerically small samples of cases, can at most serve as exploratory hypotheses for continuing research on these implementation issues. And even those researchers whose studies document successful implementation do not argue that such implementation resulted in sweeping reforms and brought about dramatic changes in conditions. Far from being a panacea, such implementation at best brought the institutions up to *minimum* constitutional standards.

THE NEED FOR EVALUATION RESEARCH

One of the first issues to be decided in formulating a research strategy is the type of research that is called for. In the case of institutional reform by decree, the model we regard as the "best fit" is evaluation research. After all, what really must be done in such cases is to determine whether a new, often comprehensive set of policies and practices are successfully implemented and, if so, to determine the results.

Having chosen evaluation research, the investigator must next determine whether formative or summative evaluation is best suited. Scriven (1967) and Weiss (1972) have discussed these two approaches to evaluation research and have distinguished between them as follows: Formative evaluation generates data and partial findings and feeds these back to program managers, implementors, policy makers, and others *as the program or project is in progress*; summative evaluation (much more like classic, basic research) produces an overall assessment of effectiveness *after completion of the project or program*. In the latter model, no tentative findings are presented in mid-project and no attempt is made to utilize the research to modify the program while it is in progress. We believe that the summative model is generally preferable in evaluating the implementation of judicial decrees in prison settings. While formative evaluation is possible in such cases, three problems pose serious obstacles to such an approach.

First, formative evaluation necessarily implies reporting information and findings back to some authority overseeing implementation. In the case of prison reform by decree, this would most likely be the court or some other official, such as a special master or a prison board. This situation makes it difficult to imagine how the researcher could achieve the cooperation of institutional management and staff beyond the mechanical cooperation that might be ordered by the court.

Second, if the master himself or herself were also the researcher, similar constraints would exist. While the master would certainly welcome incremental findings and partial conclusions as implementation progressed, the adversarial situation created by the decree would likely undermine, to a large degree, the type of cooperation necessary for good formative evaluation.

Third, by definition, court-ordered reform in a prison setting implies an adversarial relationship between the court and the organization being reformed. (This is true even if some individuals in that organization may be sympathetic to the court decree and may seek change.) Therefore, any partial finding generated by formative evaluation research which results in additional conflict between the court and the organization is likely to place the researcher on the court's side of the adversarial conflict.

Although we suggest a summative model, it poses problems which must be overcome. First, although there is no attempt to feed back preliminary results while the implementation is in progress, a researcher could be suspected of doing so. Second, the cooperation of management and staff remains problematic. Third, the researcher's role must be defined differently than that of the master, and those differences must be communicated effectively to all interested parties. Fourth, there must be established ethical guidelines for the researcher concerning the use of information about nonimplementation or the violation of prisoners' rights.

Judicial decrees can vary according to the type of adjudication, the complexity of enforcement, and the nature of the obstacles impeding implementation (Note, 1981). These differences can influence both the research methodology and the type of compliance mechanism. For example, a court order targeting a particular incident or practice (discrete adjudication) will certainly differ from an order attempting to eliminate the causes of ongoing violations (complex enforcement). Also, the nature and extent of political and other obstacles, both perceived and real, will call for different strategies.

These issues illustrate the complexity of the situation confronting such research endeavors. Although they can be resolved, it may be at the expense of the research. For example, many issues turn on the role differentiation between researcher and special master. The role of the researcher should be to assess the master's work, as well as the compliance or noncompliance behavior of the organization. Since the presence of a master is both an independent and a dependent variable in the implementation model, good research would demand that the impact of the master be measured to the fullest extent possible.

Likewise, the researcher, even though he or she may certainly have personal views concerning the merits of the decree and the desirability of seeing it implemented, is not there to enforce the decree, but to evaluate its enforcement. Failure to recognize this distinction would be critical to the study. This does *not* mean that the researcher must be value-neutral, which is to say inhuman. Rather, he or she must establish systematic research questions and procedures, develop multiple indicators of outcome, and stick to those as closely as possible without being obtrusive within the organization. To do otherwise would be to engender conflict which might alter the nature of the implementation process, perhaps endangering it, and would lead to a situation where the researcher would very likely have difficulty in establishing and maintaining the necessary rapport with all parties. Especially in a prison environment it is quite easy to become labeled as either the court's agent or the administration's agent, since the principal actors usually are fully committed to a zero-sum view of the world inside the walls.

A more perplexing issue is that of the legal, ethical, and moral obligations of a researcher who, in the course of evaluating the implementation process, discovers evidence of willful noncompliance by prison authorities or staff or the violation of prisoners' rights. In this hypothetical situation, there can be no simple and predetermined solution. We can only suggest that one useful maxim might be to overlook minor transgressions and inform the court about major violations, if observed.

To summarize this portion of the discussion, summative evaluation is a more appropriate research model than is formative evaluation for the assessment of decree implementation in correctional settings. However, numerous problems exist which complicate the researcher's ability to engage even in summative evaluation. Despite these problems, it would appear that the need to generate new knowledge about the implementation process and the organizational dynamics associated with successful or unsuccessful implementation justifies the investment of substantial research planning in overcoming these obstacles.

Finally, we believe that it is completely appropriate for the researcher to guarantee anonymity to the organization, its administration and staff, and the special master in exchange for access to detailed information about the implementation process. The research, to be published and disseminated on completion of the study, would disguise all of the specific information and would concentrate instead on what happened and how generalizable it might be in constructing a theory of implementation. If such guarantees of anonymity are necessary to ensure cooperation and to enable researchers to carry out high-level inquiries, then the tradeoff is acceptable. This guarantee of anonymity should not, however, extend to any criminal acts observed or learned by the researcher.

THEORETICAL AND METHODOLOGICAL ISSUES

Several important theoretical and methodological issues may be of importance to those contemplating the type of research we have discussed. First, with respect to theory, both complex organizational theory and the systems-analytic perspective are useful organizing frameworks in the conduct of research of this nature. Organizational and systems theories help us understand which variables might be selected for empirical analysis during the implementation process. These include:

(1) the changing roles and power structure of the organization/system,
(2) the changing patterns of allocation of monetary and human resources,
(3) changes in the stated missions or goals,
(4) changes in policies, and
(5) changes in procedures.

Even when using such empirical indicators, the researcher must constantly be aware that the implementation is proceeding in a sociopolitical context. Certain goal conflicts in corrections must be considered as to the effects that such conflict may have on the implementation of change. Other constraints, such as structural role conflicts, may also be important impediments. For example, in evaluating the implementation of a jail reform decree, the researcher must keep in mind that in the great majority of American cities and counties there is no structural advocate for local jails. The budget for jails is almost always a part of the sheriff's or police chief's law enforcement budget, and there are powerful political incentives to allocate those funds for highly visible law enforcement (e.g., more patrol cars on the street). Conversely, there is little incentive (other than personal conviction or court orders) to allocate much of that law enforcement budget to the invisible arena of the jail, especially when many citizens would regard such expenditures as inappropriate, since the inmates are often perceived as deserving whatever they get (even those who have not yet stood trial).

Methodologically, perhaps the most important issue, other than simply getting permission to conduct the research and getting the principals involved to cooperate with the data collection efforts, is that of developing systematic data collection procedures and multiple indicators, both of which should be designed to ensure a representative sample of organizational behavior and more than one way of assessing success or failure.

IMPLICATIONS

Research on the implementation of judicial decrees in corrections or any other institutional setting can contribute both to knowledge and the application of knowledge. Such studies should offer excellent opportunities to test and refine theories of implementation and organizational behavior, insights into comparative management strategies which might facilitate or inhibit implementation, and research challenges which afford the opportunity to develop innovative field methods and analytic procedures.

Finally, if successfully carried out, summative research on such implementation may still be used in one formative sense: That is, the dissemination of the findings of such studies should include the judiciary, either via informal contacts with them or through formal continuing education for judges. Judges typically receive very little formal training relating to organizational behavior. If they are to improve the prospects for meaningful correctional reform through law, they must become more sophisticated in their understanding of the implementation process and the dynamics of organizations targeted for change.

NOTES

1. Courts are adopting various methods "to provide themselves with appropriate instruments required for the performance of their duties" (ex parte Peterson, 1920). Under this rule, courts can require compliance in a uniform manner, but enforcement techniques often vary.

2. Justice Marshall, joined in dissent by Justice Brennan in Jones v. North Carolina Prisoners' Labor Union, Inc. (1977), provided several examples of such inconsistencies in the Supreme Court's deference to the expertise of penal administrators. Also see Rhodes v. Chapman (1981) for a recent example of the Supreme Court's return to a "hands-off" position, in contrast to the more aggressive, interventionist stance of some federal district courts.

CASES

BANNING v. LOONEY (1954) 348 U.S. 859
COFFIN v. REICHARD (1944) 143 F. 2d 443, 445
EX PARTE PETERSON (1920) 253 U.S. 300, 312-313
JONES v. NORTH CAROLINA PRISONERS' LABOR UNION, INC. (1977) 443, U.S. 119
MORRIS v. TRAVISONO (1970) 310 F. Supp. 857 (D.R.I.)
PRICE v. JOHNSTON (1948) 334 U.S. 266, 285-286
RHODES v. CHAPMAN (1981) 101 S. Ct. 2392
RUFFIN v. VIRGINIA (1871) 62 Va. (21 Gratt) 790, 796

REFERENCES

ALEXANDER, E. (1978) "The new prison administrators and the court: new directions in prison law." Texas Law Rev. 56: 963-1008.

BECKER, L. and M. M. FEELEY [eds.] (1975) The Impact of Supreme Court Decisions. New York: Oxford Univ. Press.

CHAMPAGNE, A. and K. C. HAAS (1976) "The impact of Johnson v. Avery on prison administration." Tennessee Law Rev. 43: 275-303.

CONNER, R. F. and C. R. HUFF (1979) Attorneys as Activists: Evaluating the American Bar Association's BASICS Program. Beverly Hills, CA: Sage.

HAAS, K. C. and A. CHAMPAGNE (1976) "The impact of Johnson v. Avery on prison administration." Tennessee Law Rev. 43: 275-303.

HARRIS, M. K. and D. P. SPILLER, Jr. (1977) After Decision: Implementation of Judicial Decrees in Correctional Settings. Washington, DC: National Institute of Law Enforcement and Criminal Justice.

Harvard Center for Criminal Justice (1972) "Judicial intervention in prison discipline." J. of Criminal Law, Criminology and Police Science 63: 200-228.

KATZ, E. (1965) "Patterns of compliance with the Schempp decision." J. of Public Law 14: 396-405.

KRISLOV, S. [ed.] (1972) Compliance and the Law. Beverly Hills, CA: Sage.

MILLER, A. S. (1965) "On the need for 'impact analysis' of supreme court decisions." Georgetown Law J. 53: 365-401.

NATHAN, V. (1979) "The use of masters in institutional reform litigation." Univ. of Toledo Law Rev. 10: 419-464.

Note (1981) "Complex enforcement: unconstitutional prison conditions." Harvard Law Rev. 94: 626-646.

RUBIN, H. T. (1976) The Courts: Fulcrum of the Justice System. Santa Monica, CA: Goodyear.

SCRIVEN, M. (1967) "The methodology of evaluation," as cited by C. H. Weiss (1972) Evaluation Research: Methods of Assessing Program Effectiveness. Englewood Cliffs, NJ: Prentice-Hall.

THOMAS, C. W. (1980) "The impotence of correctional law," pp. 243-260 in G. P. Alpert (ed.) Legal Rights of Prisoners. Beverly Hills, CA: Sage.

WASBY, S. L. (1970) The Impact of the United States Supreme Court. Homewood, IL: Dorsey Press.

WEISS, C. H. (1972) Evaluation Research: Methods of Assessing Program Effectiveness. Englewood Cliffs, NJ: Prentice-Hall.

WILLIE, C. and S. GREENBLATT [eds.] (1981) Community Politics and Educational Change. New York: Longmans.

ABOUT THE AUTHORS

GEOFFREY P. ALPERT is Director of the Center for Study of Law and Society, University of Miami. He received his Ph.D. from Washington State University in sociology and attended law school at the University of Oregon. He is currently doing research on the interplay between the rights of prisoners and the rights of prison guards, and on the impact of Haitians and Cubans on the criminal justice system in South Florida.

CRAIG H. BLAKELY is Assistant Professor of Psychology at Michigan State University, where he earned his Ph.D. in 1981. He was a Research Associate with the Adolescent Diversion Project from 1977 through 1980. He is currently Director of the Implementation Research Project at Michigan State University's Center for Innovation Research.

TIMOTHY S. BYNUM received his Ph.D. in criminology from Florida State University and is currently an associate professor in the School of Criminal Justice at Michigan State University. His prior research has focused on the impact of extralegal factors in police and parole decisions. He is currently involved in a study of the variation in juvenile detention practices in the state of Michigan.

WILLIAM S. DAVIDSON II is Associate Professor of Psychology at Michigan State University. He earned his Ph.D. at the University of Illinois at Urbana-Champaign, where he has been Research Associate at the Community Psychology Action Center. Davidson has also been Director of Kentfields Rehabilitation Program. He received the 1976 Watson-Wilson Consultation Research Award from the American Psychological Association's Division of Consulting Psychology. Davidson is co-author of *In Response to Aggression* with A. Goldstein, E. Carr, and P. Wehr.

SCOTT H. DECKER is Associate Professor of Administration of Justice and Research Fellow in the Center for Metropolitan Studies, University of Missouri-St. Louis. He received his M.A. and Ph.D. in criminology from Florida State University. His published works have focused on minorities and the administration of justice, evaluations of alternative police strategies, and alternative measures of crime. He is currently involved in analyzing the results of a juvenile diversion program and a time-series examination of the death penalty.

JACK R. GREENE is Associate Professor in the School of Criminal Justice at Michigan State University. He received a B.S. in criminal justice from Northeastern University, an M.S. in criminal justice, and a Ph.D. in social science from Michigan State University. His research has focused on policy and organizational analyses in public policing. He has published several articles on police and organizational related matters in a number of academic journals, and recently edited *Managing Police Work* (Sage, 1982).

JOAN NEFF GURNEY is Assistant Professor of Sociology and Coordinator of the Area Studies Program in Criminal Justice at the University of Richmond. She received her B.A. in sociology from the University of Delaware (1974) and her M.A. and Ph.D. from Ohio State University (1976, 1980). Her current research interests include organizational deviance, inequality within the criminal justice system, and community treatment programs for adult and juvenile offenders. She is currently conducting research on juvenile diversion programs in Virginia. Her most recent publication is a critical analysis of the relative deprivation concept in social movements theory and research (*The Sociological Quarterly*).

C. RONALD HUFF is Associate Professor of Public Administration and Sociology and Director of the Program for the Study of Crime and Delinquency at Ohio State University. He received his M.S.W. from the University of Michigan and Ph.D. in sociology from Ohio State University. He has published extensively, served as an associate editor of *Criminology*, and held a position on the executive board of the American Society of Criminology.

MERRY MORASH is Assistant Professor at the School of Criminal Justice, Michigan State University. Her Ph.D. is from the Institute of Criminal Justice and Criminology at the University of Maryland. Her research interests include juvenile delinquency, and she has co-authored the forthcoming edition of *Juvenile Delinquency: Concepts and Control* with Robert Trojanowicz. Additional research in progress focuses on the utility of LEAA publications in promoting the implementation of criminal justice policies.

LUCY Y. STEINITZ, Ph.D., is Director of Client Services at Jewish Family & Children's Service of Baltimore, Maryland. She received her Ph.D. from the University of Chicago's School of Social Service Administration, and is currently revising her dissertation for book publication under the title, *Two Islands—Churches and Community Service Organizations Among the Elderly*. The investigative research on which this chapter is based was conducted while Dr. Steinitz was a Research Fellow at the University of Chicago's Center for the Study of Welfare Policy in Washington, D.C., 1980 through 1981.

MARVIN ZALMAN is Chairman of the Criminal Justice Department at Wayne State University. As Project Leader of the Michigan Felony Sentencing Project and as policy consultant to the Michigan Supreme Court, he has been involved in research and policy development in the area of criminal sentencing. His current research interests include sentencing policy and the exploration of sociocultural bases of criminal law. He holds a J.D. from Brooklyn Law School and a Ph.D. from the School of Criminal Justice of the State University of New York at Albany. He is listed in *Who's Who in American Law*, 2nd Ed.